Rachel -

I pray this speaks to your
heart where the words
need to dwell.

God's
Peace
Julie

Numbers
6: 24-26

Streams of Light from a
HEART BROKEN

Hopeful Reflections on a
Grief-Shadowed Journey

JULIE GRANT

WESTBOW
PRESS®
A DIVISION OF THOMAS NELSON
& ZONDERVAN

WestBow Press books may be ordered through booksellers or by contacting:

WestBow Press
A Division of Thomas Nelson & Zondervan
1663 Liberty Drive
Bloomington, IN 47403
www.westbowpress.com
844-714-3454

Cover design/Author photo: Aaron Grant
Cover photo: Julie Grant

ISBN: 978-1-6642-5818-1 (sc)
ISBN: 978-1-6642-5819-8 (e)

Print information available on the last page.

WestBow Press rev. date: 03/17/2022

To my sons, Daniel and Aaron, who share with
me a heart broken, and to
our heavenly Father, who gently
pieces us back together.

Introduction

As an ER nurse for thirty-two years, I understand death. I have seen death at its most horrific, most shocking, and most senseless level. I have also seen patients whose last countenances bear the very manifestation of peace. I understand death as it pertains to the family desperately trying to process the information that their loved one has not survived. I have seen this played out violently as well as in total silence. I now understand death in a totally different way, in a personal way. I know how death can completely turn your whole world on its axis, leaving you feeling somehow farther from light and more affected by the pull of gravity. Overcoming the inertia that is grief, to complete even the smallest task, is overwhelming. Breathing is exhausting. Thinking, if done at all, seems stuck in a downward spiral from which extrication is impossible.

My husband, John, died suddenly and unexpectedly nearly three years ago. In the early days, the raw days, there was not a second of time that my entire life wasn't processed through the lens of grief. Every facet of my being was consumed. Grief was not the tidy, linear process that I had studied. In this dark realm of chaos, I found there was only one thing I could do: Cry. Out. To. Jesus. I cried out to Him with constant prayers of guttural pleadings to carry me through each moment in time. Walking every step through that valley with Jesus was intentional. The path was difficult; it was often completely overwhelming. Yet it was so worth it. Writing about the journey and sharing my thoughts while in the midst of it was like the slow folding of that ever-present shroud of grief. It allowed me to compact it in to a form that fits in my heart and can be carried with me, neither overwhelming nor overburdening as greatly as it once did. These are those writings, pieces of my heart that I shared.

Grieving is a process that takes time and effort and intentionality. It is different for each person because each person's grief is so vastly different. I think when people talk about the work of grieving, this is what they are talking about. It is not just saying a prayer occasionally or reading your Bible more. It is allowing yourself to be present and even totally consumed by your grief for a time. It is living through the lens of grief while grieving through the lens of faith that enables us to move forward with our grief. This is the most important work we can do because, in the end, it isn't only about the grieving, it is about the living; It is about finding the goodness and beauty that still exist in the world and celebrating them with your one life.

PART 1

· · · · · · · · · · ·

Being Held

This was playing on my way to work as the sun
rose pink in the morning sky. Sigh.
'Cause I'll be by your side wherever you fall
In the dead of night whenever you call
And please don't fight these hands that are holding you
My hands are holding you. ("By Your Side," Tenth Avenue North)[1]

My readings today have all reminded me to remain
present in His presence, to be still in His grace. And
not to fight His hands that truly hold me.

Thy Will Be Done

No one who ever said to God, "Thy will be done," and
meant it with his heart, ever failed to find joy—not just in
heaven, or even down the road in the future in this world,
but in this world at that very moment. (Peter Kreeft)

Thy. Will. Be. Done. Four small words that can change a life when they
represent the posture in which it is lived. Thirteen months ago, at this very
moment actually, I was proclaiming the goodness of God to a church full of
people who had come to celebrate John's life with us. Yes, thirteen months.
Just like in new life, new death is marked in smaller increments of time—by
days, by hours, by seconds, by breaths—each representing a "victory" over
grief.

I don't know what triggered these thoughts this morning, but I remember
walking around the block that morning and being in an almost trancelike
state, uttering prayers for the words for John's eulogy and the strength to get
through it. I am horrible at speaking in front of crowds, and tears coming
can shut my throat up tight. Oh, how I was praying, those moaning prayers
that come from deep within your spirit. What came to me immediately and
repeatedly was not what I had expected but what I knew in my heart to be
true: "God is good—all the time." It seemed to be such a strange message to
proclaim within a few days of John's having been fully alive and then taken
so suddenly. Yet from the very beginning of this journey, I have felt that this
is the message God wants me to proclaim, to embrace, to live out. From that
very dark place of initial shock, I was able to let go, to yield to His will, to
declare Him good. Whenever I feel mired in doubt or the "whys" try to spill
from my eyes, there has always been an acceptance of God's sovereignty,
goodness, and grace.

The reward I have received has been, indeed, an inexplicable joy. Joy doesn't negate the other emotions encountered in loss; I think it is a thread that can be delicately intertwined within all these emotions. Theopedia.com describes joy as, "a state of mind and an orientation of the heart. It is a settled state of contentment, confidence, and hope." I think it is also the posture of the soul, the yielding of a life.

Thy will be done. (Matthew 6:10 KJV)

Personal Reflection

God is GOOD ~ ALL the time!

The First Week

Time is passing so strangely right now. It has been a week. It seems much longer in that I don't understand how we could have experienced all we have in just one week. It also seems much shorter because we are so raw. The outpouring of love and friendship has been so amazing in helping us heal. We have a strange peace; I know that comes from God. I also think, and we discussed this at John's bedside, that it comes from having no regrets. We are blessed that there were no harbored angers, unforgiveness, or words left unspoken. We always spoke our love. Right before Daniel left for Colorado, we were playing cards, and John just stopped and told our sons how proud he was of them, of the young men they had become. What a gift! God is bringing beauty from the ashes.

John was an organ donor, and his gift may change the lives of more than fifty people. Wow! That gave us such joy. Knowing his gift could keep someone else from experiencing what we are going through, even for a short time, blessed us. The celebration of John's life was so uplifting. We all knew what a great guy he was; apparently it wasn't a very well-kept secret. So many people! God was moving in a big way. I was so thankful that I could speak. I had so many people praying that my throat wouldn't close up, and I wouldn't send a blubbering, squeaky message. I prayed for the words and the voice; I felt like those prayers were answered. It was wonderful to see so many people who were important to both of us.

We are taking one day at a time, one step at a time, sometimes one breath at a time. We have ventured from our cocoon out into the world as a tight little unit with eyes averted downward to avoid eye contact and a possible public spectacle. This has been effective and has the bonus of finding a lot of coins on the ground! We are healing; we are allowing ourselves to laugh and be joyful. We are so thankful for all the prayers and cards and food. I feel Jesus walking this walk very closely with me. I heard this song by Matthew West this morning, and I thought it was appropriate.

> Now I'm just a beggar in the presence of a King
> I wish I could bring so much more
> But if it's true, You use broken things
> Then here I am Lord, I'm all Yours.[2]

Personal Reflection

God is GOOD ~ ALL the time!

Be Aware of the Why

My son Aaron and I were talking last night and thinking that this really makes no sense. John was so healthy and loved and just all around great. His light is missed in a world that already possesses too much darkness. I told Aaron I had been thinking about this, too, and I think it is very dangerous to get stuck in the why. I think the why is like emotional and spiritual quicksand. Satan can live in that dark place and pull you under. We all know people stuck in the why. They can't get past the question, "Why me?" I don't know that I will ever get that answer. I pray that God will reveal to me how He turns this into beauty. Yet I understand that He may not.

I think this is the time to ask God to show us "How." How can I keep moving forward with faith in His plan? How can I have peace in my sorrow? How can I trust Him? Those are the conversations we are currently having. Keep the prayers coming! We can feel them strengthening us!

> Guide me in your truth and teach me, for you are God my
> Savior, and my hope is in you all day long. (Psalm 25:5)

Personal Reflection

God is GOOD ~ ALL the time!

Trust

You know how sometimes you encounter the same reading or theme over and over and over? I don't believe in coincidences, so I kind of perk up when this happens and try to figure out what message I am supposed to be getting. For me this week it has been Romans 8. I am twenty-two weeks into my Bible reading program, and Romans 8 was one of the readings this week. It was also the reading this week in my women's study group. Romans 8:28 was the key verse for the study:

> And we know that in *all* things God works for the *good* of those who love him, who have been called according to his purpose. (emphasis added)

This verse was also read yesterday at the celebration of Claudia's life. Claudia is the eighteen-year-old, beautiful, bright light of a daughter of my good friend Angie. She was tragically taken in a car accident this week. But there again in this time of sorrow are those words "all" and "good" surrounding God. And while this verse was popping up everywhere this week, life was also hitting hard at every turn with sickness and death and worry and fear. And now a flipping hurricane! So I have been processing this and asking for Solomon's discernment and wisdom (another theme of my week)!

The reading in church today was from Mark 7, and Father Hal emphasized verse 37: "He [Jesus] has done *all* things well." He reminded us that our job is to *trust* in every moment and *believe* in Him because, you guessed it, he threw some Romans 8:28 at us! He reminded us that when Jesus pours His Spirit upon us, nothing is impossible!

What hit me this morning was that these are all just words on paper if you don't believe them, lean on them, and trust in them. Our hope hinges on trusting that God is good all the time and that He is the *only* one who can bring beauty from ashes. I am praying hard for my amazing friend during this time.

Personal Reflection

God is GOOD ~ ALL the time!

One Month In

I cannot believe it has been a month. As Aaron said, some moments feel as if we have been dragging through this time for a year. At other times, it feels as though we are right back in the hospital. Everything seems that way, a dichotomy of emotions coming rapid-fire at any given moment. I question why it was so easy to trade in John's truck, yet his toothbrush is still next to mine on the sink. Why do I feel so close to him at times and completely alone at others? I know that our little lives are so insignificant in the grand scheme of the universe, yet I know with all I am that the Creator of that universe is weeping with us. I am hopeful to see what God has planned for our lives and what beauty and joy will come. Yet I am saddened that I won't be able to experience it all with my love. Yes, I am still all over the place, but my feet are firmly on the rock of my faith. I heard the song "Thy Will" by Hillary Scott this morning, and it brought me to my knees.

> Sometimes I have to stop
> Remember that You're God and I am not.[3]

('Cause I would have done this part of life a lot differently!)

Personal Reflection

God is GOOD ~ ALL the time!

The Dance

Yesterday was my first day back to work. During these past few weeks, Daniel, Aaron, and I have truly appreciated the time we have had to bond together away from constant reminders of the missing piece of our heart. The North Carolina mountains and Colorado offered some joy and some beautifully poignant memories, along with many winks from God on the animal front. I was really hoping for a moose, but then when the llamas appeared—now that was priceless. Once again God shows He knows what I need better than I do. I also learned, too, that apparently I cannot get near a flowing river without some deep guttural emotion bubbling up within me. Who knew? These are all memories I will cherish forever.

I am, however, a creature of habit. And as such, I thrive on a routine. I was not prepared for how tough that first morning was going to be, though—how closely linked to John it has always been. Mornings were like a well-choreographed dance. I quietly arose in the dark and made my way to the shower on tiptoe. John came in when I was just about finished and took his turn. There was always a, "Good morning," and a, "How did you sleep?" but not much chatter. We took our places at the sinks, a little leg pat from me to move him a tad so I could open my drawer; the same from him so he could open his. Either the drawers got wider through the years or we did!

A couple of months ago, in the middle of that dance, I paused and was struck by the feeling that this ritual was very intimate and precious. It was like God was saying, "Take a breath, take a snapshot, and keep this memory forever." That exact moment is crystal clear in my mind. Yesterday I tried to shake things up. I thought, *I will turn on lights and read a bit before the shower and play music loudly!* That didn't go so well. This song was playing. I have always loved this song, but it never felt quite so personal:

9

Cry Out to Jesus
To everyone who's lost someone they love
Long before it was their time
You feel like the days you had were not enough
When you said goodbye ...
There is hope for the helpless
Rest for the weary
Love for the broken heart
Cry out to Jesus, Cry out. (Third Day)[4]

Personal Reflection

God is GOOD ~ ALL the time!

Thoughts for Today

I decided to try to read before sleep … like normal. Maybe it would bring on better sleep. I opened my book to the place marked with a piece of paper. The paper had notes from when I shared at small group two weeks ago. I had spoken about things that happened, which were like secret signals from God letting me know He was here, very present, walking closely. For the past year, for me it has been bunnies. But when I think back, bunnies have always brought smiles to me. I told the story about when John and I were in the mountains about ten years ago. Our room overlooked a small meadow, and I remarked that it was so sweet but just needed a little bunny nibbling on the grass. The words had no sooner come out of my mouth than a bunny was catapulted out of the woods next to the meadow. He didn't crawl out or even hop gently. It was like he was hurled out. Then he sat quietly and nibbled grass; the bucolic scene was now perfect. We laughed aloud. I thought God got a kick out of that. Either that or we were indeed in *The Matrix*. Then just a few days before small group, we were walking by the lake, and I remarked that I hadn't seen the deer out there for quite a while. I wondered aloud if the fox family was maybe keeping them away. Immediately after I spoke, a deer ran straight toward us and then turned into the woods. The reason she was running? She was being chased by a fox. Stunned laughter ensued. I could see God getting a kick out of it too. I believe God delights in bringing us joy. And if He delights in being part of our everyday journeys with those little things, we must be assured He has our back with the big stuff.

> May God, the Giver of hope, fill you with continual joy and
> peace because you trust in Him. (Romans 15:13 WNT)

I was walking in the same place with a friend a few days later and talking to her about this. She told me about a book she had seen, *When God Winks at You: How God Speaks Directly to You through the Power of Coincidence* by Squire Rushnell.

Wow! a "Godwink." now it had a name. I love it! Of course I bought the book. My recollection is that the author describes a Godwink as that favorite person who catches your eye across the chaos of life and gives you a reassuring wink, just to let you know that he sees you; he's got your back. God cares deeply about everything we are going through.

So I smiled, remembering the small-group meeting and thinking about how much God has been winking since John has gone. Many people are sharing how they have seen Him moving through all this. My friend Carol said, "I think God has Tourette's from all of this winking!" That made me laugh. Then I read the first sentence on the page of the book I am reading: "Listen carefully: Suffering will try to separate you from Jesus. You must not let it." All righty then. Message received.

Personal Reflection

God is GOOD ~ ALL the time!

Derailed ... Or Not

The past couple weeks have been kind of rough. Before we ever left the hospital, I looked both boys in their eyes and told them that they could not allow this loss to derail their lives. We would push forward together, just like their daddy would have wanted. We Are ... Grant Strong! #noregrets! That was our mantra. Then Daniel said "Well I am not going back to physician assistant (PA) school." He had gotten increasingly ambivalent about this transition in recent months. We had talked before he left about how much he loved coaching and working with youth. He had said he would work as a PA for ten or so years to make some money, and then he could pursue coaching full time. I remember feeling sad at that revelation. Five years ago, Daniel embarked on the journey to be a PA. It was at the center of every choice he made—classes he took, Peace Corps assignments, applying to schools, working in the ER. Yet embedded in each of these experiences he found himself working with youth.

Daniel is very goal oriented, and to let go of a goal is difficult; it feels like failure to him. However, he had felt uneasy about this even as he was leaving for Colorado. So when we called him on the first day of classes with this horrible news, to Daniel that was a clear sign. When he told me of his decision, I was at peace with it, especially after a couple of days of talking with him and praying about it. I look back over the past two years and can clearly see God revealing to Daniel what his path should be. Actually, the things he has been doing over the past five years have prepared him perfectly for this new path.

I think the thing that was hardest this week was coming to terms with Aaron's decision to withdraw from classes. I don't know why that was like a gut punch to me. I certainly knew he didn't feel ready to go back to school;

he had been quite clear about that all summer. Actually, he told anyone who would listen. But he is the baby and I, I was determined that he was not going to sit at home in his underwear and play Fortnite for the semester. "Idle hands are a devil's workshop," one of Grandma Minnie's favorites. I thought that once he got up there and started classes, he would be busy and distracted, and that would keep him moving forward on the "right" path. Everyone knows sitting in Spanish class is clearly going to keep you focused—said no one ever! Now this is where it gets tough. To try to help me understand this, Aaron said, "If I were to die tomorrow, [gulp], I will never have lived the life I see for myself." That really struck me. When I strip it all down, it's the truth. Aaron has been diligently on the course his daddy and I set for him and tied him to, even though it has never felt like a good fit for him. We encouraged him to keep plugging along, having total faith that we knew what was best for Aaron. I think the problem for me is that I am more like Daniel in that I establish a goal and work toward it in a systematic manner. Aaron is creative, a dreamer. I cannot envision his dreams, and I don't see the exact path that he has in his mind's eye. That scares me; it feels like freefall to my nature. So I must trust.

Through this time of John's loss, God has been whispering to me, "Trust Me," in every imaginable way—through song, readings, cards, and scripture. Here's the thing. I *do* trust God! I long ago released Him from the Julie-sized box I had Him in for most of my faith journey. I have loved seeing how great and wide and deep are His love and power and wisdom. I marvel at these things daily. I am grateful for all my many blessings. I trust His plan for my life, even though it is clearly so different than my plan. My plan involved growing old with my best friend, enjoying walks and talks and laughter each day along the way. I can even let go of that and trust. But I am having a really hard time trusting Him with my sons. Yes, the sons that He gave me! I trust Him to tend to the immensity of the universe, but my babies? Paradoxically, that seems so much more difficult. Releasing that grip makes me feel as if I am shirking my parental responsibilities. Yet as we raise our children, I think we are meant to release our grips gradually on their lives. I remember loosening a little when they started walking and exploring their world away from my watchful eye, and again when they went to school. And especially when they started to drive and went to college. I was not prepared to release them completely, to trust that God had them, until ... Well, I don't know when exactly!

After praying and thinking about this for the past couple weeks, I do know that I have found that peace again. I do know that trust is letting go. I will probably have to do this every single day for a while. I would be lying if I said it is done with hands wide open and raised to heaven. But at least I have released my iron grip on my sons' lives. Isn't that the first step in letting go and letting God?

Personal Reflection

God is GOOD ~ ALL the time!

Mountaintops in Valleys

When I was eleven years old, I lived with my grandparents on the island of Borneo for a little over a year. Weekends we sometimes headed out to one of the nearby uncharted islands with a few Filipino families. It was like a wonderland. I discovered the refreshment of green coconut water and its slippery, sweet meat. I accidentally dropped my pineapple in the sea and discovered it tasted even better. I grilled over a fire a fish that had just been plucked from the end of a spear. The most magical part was snorkeling above the reefs. The water was perfectly clear, and the coral reefs were more spectacular than any I had ever seen or have seen since—giant clams, fish of every imaginable color and design, and the rocks alive with colorful sponges, anemones, urchins, and an abundance of other organisms. Even the best aquarium exhibits I have seen pale in comparison. It's funny how we experience so many things on life's journey, and they become the pinnacles to which we compare any future similar encounters. We strive to find or even exceed that mark. We are content with nothing less.

I have experienced the same thing in my faith journey. I found a church in California the summer after my freshman year in college, and it was exactly what I needed to start to grow my faith. That church became a reference point to which I compared all subsequent churches. I had been to the mountaintop. I had encountered Jesus in the church and nothing else will suffice. I have had a few of those mountaintop experiences along the way, those times when you feel like your Creator is just a whisper away. I remember after my Cursillo renewal weekend, I couldn't speak about it at the closing ceremony because I was a pregnant, blubbering mess. John had said that his whole life's religious experience had been based on knowing *about* Jesus, but after that weekend, he felt like it was the first time he really *knew* Jesus.

Today marks three months since I had to say goodbye to the love of my life, the sweetest guy a girl could love, and the best daddy ever. This is by far the deepest valley I have had to travel through in my life. What I never expected, however, was that in this very dark place I would find the light and love of God in such a profoundly intimate way. All I had to do was call to Him and run into His arms. He continues to hold me tightly.

Personal Reflection

God is GOOD ~ ALL the time!

Land Mines

This has been a good week. There has been more joy than sorrow. That is not to say that I haven't encountered a few land mines on the path that leave me in a state of joyful melancholy. Land mines are the things that can just take you down. The song that instantly triggers the sweetest memory. Or the accidental click of the mouse that starts playing the video you were not prepared to watch but cannot stop watching, smiling through tears throughout the playing. Oh, how I miss the way joy just crept right out of John's eyes.

Sometimes with grief you just have to lean into it, and let it take you, remembering that Jesus wept too (John 11:35). I have tried to narrow my focus, savoring the sweetness of the journey and who I am journeying with. Trusting where He is taking me, how He is transforming my life. It is scary to let go, especially for this future-focused, forever-planning girl. I was mulling all this over while mowing the lawn today when I heard the song "Somewhere in the Middle" by Casting Crowns.

> Somewhere between the wrong and the right
> Somewhere between the darkness and the light
> Somewhere between who I was and who you're making me
> Somewhere in the middle, you'll find me
> Just how close can I get, Lord, to my surrender without losing all control.[5]

I don't think I am the only one who wants to surrender but is afraid of losing all control. That line always hits me between the eyes. The thing that I have learned recently, though, is that control is an illusion, a mirage. We really have no control over the big, important things—life, death, hurricanes, tsunamis. We only have control over the choices we make. Will we choose laughter or tears, faith or fear, love or hate? I know for me, I will choose to cling to Philippians 4:13 (NKJV): "I can do all things through Christ who strengthens me." And in that place I hope to find joy for the moment.

Personal Reflection

God is GOOD ~ ALL the time!

All Our Days

All the days ordained for me were written in your book
before one of them came to be. (Psalm 139:16)

During the past week or so, this verse has been turning up everywhere—podcasts, referenced in readings, GriefShare homework, note cards, and even in the book I was reading last night. It doesn't completely surprise me in that it was a verse I clung to in the early days of this walk. It helped me to make sense of the fact that although it was never going to make sense to me, John had lived the days that had been ordained for him. It is a comfort in a way. It reminds me not to overthink the details of that day and just leave it in God's hands. I can trust the One who numbered the stars to bring order to my little world.

I have shared this thought with John's organ recipients as well, trying to allay any guilt that they may have. I do not believe John died so that they could live. I believe he had completed his ordained days. Their receipt of new lives was the work of God bringing light out of darkness in such a miraculous way.

I am just not sure why I am getting this verse so much now. Maybe it's to remind me that no amount of worrying or planning or micromanaging is going to add a single day to my life. Maybe it's so I reflect on the fact God knows me intimately. That is pretty mind-blowing if you ever just ponder it. Maybe it's because He wants me to remember that this verse isn't just meant to bring comfort in death but also a hope for life. I can walk in peace and joy with my God for all my ordained days, and that is good.

Personal Reflection

God is GOOD ~ ALL the time!

Soul-ular Changes

It has been very hard to try to convey how changed I feel since John's death. The boys and I have talked about it, and I can remember saying things like, "I feel so different, like I am somehow altered at a very deep, physical level—a cellular level—all the way to my DNA." I just feel deeply and profoundly transformed somehow. I feel John's presence with me, not in a ghostly, creeping around the house kind of way, but in a spiritual way, like he has become even more a part of who I am than when he was alive. It is weird and hard to explain.

I recently read an essay by Henri J. M. Nouwen in his book, *The Inner Voice of Love*, and this spoke to me: "When the place where God dwells in you is intimately connected with the place where God dwells in the other, the absence of the other person is not destructive. On the contrary, it will challenge you to enter more deeply into communion with God, the source of all unity and communion among people." Then he goes on, "The pain you experience from the death or absence of the person you love, then, always calls you to a deeper knowledge of God's love. God's love is all the love you need, and it reveals to you the love of God in the other. So, the God in you can speak to the God in the other. This is deep speaking to deep, a mutuality in the heart of God, who embraces both of you."[6] Wow! The heart of God embracing us both. What a beautiful image. Our connectedness through God becomes stronger as we seek God during tough times. I wasn't too far off in my thinking; the changes I have been feeling aren't cellular but soul-ular!

Aaron read this essay, too, and we were discussing this whole idea. He had an interesting thought: Maybe the love that comes from this deep place of interconnectedness with God and each other is God's way of giving us a tiny glimpse of what heaven will be like. Smile.

It is well, it is well with my soul.

Personal Reflection

God is GOOD ~ ALL the time!

Anniversary Dates

Monday marked five months. I don't understand why anniversary days seem harder somehow. It really makes no logical sense. It is not like John's laughter is missed more than on every other day. It is not like our drive-by hugs and swift kisses in passing are any more absent. It was the perfect day too—cold, rainy, gloomy—a clear reflection of my heart as I trudged into the ER and through another day without my best friend. It didn't help that God and I started out the day in a heated discussion. I wasn't really asking why; I know I may not ever know the answer to that question. It was more about me wanting to see some of this supposed good that was coming out of all of this, me responding to Him that I did *not* consider it pure joy to face this trial (James 1:2, paraphrased), as I had just read in my morning devotion. It was me stomping around with a poked-out lip. Yes, just picture any toddler not getting his or her way!

I was kind of praying and processing this through the morning when I was told I had a visitor in the break room. Since I was already just barely keeping it together, it was no surprise that tears flowed as soon as I entered the break room and recognized one of the nurses who had taken care of John in the hospital. She had been so kind and empathetic and professional in her care of him, of us. She had driven about an hour to bring lunch and let me know that she often thought about and prayed for our family. During her visit she revealed that her brother had drowned shortly before she cared for John and that our family really touched her heart. It struck me that in some way God had used us at the lowest, darkest place we had ever been. He used us to touch her heart in some way that I cannot even fathom. She works in neuro ICU and takes care of many patients and families, but God used *our* family. She brought her mom and aunt with her on this visit, and I apologized a bit for the flood of tears and explained it was an anniversary day. Her mom, still grieving the loss of her son, gave me a hug and said, "It sometimes just overcomes us. It's our new normal." At that point I smiled as that is exactly what I have written on the front of the journal I am keeping.

So once again there was me questioning His plan, and once again Him reminding me that He's got me. Then, as if that wasn't enough, the proud new owner of one of John's kidneys sent me a text to let me know she was thinking about me. Sigh. I just love it when God shows off.

Personal Reflection

God is GOOD ~ ALL the time!

Blessed Be the Name of the Lord

Let thankfulness temper all your thoughts. A thankful mind-set keeps you in touch with Me ... Gratitude enables you to see the Light of My Presence shining on all our circumstances. Cultivate a thankful heart, for this glorifies Me and fills you with Joy.[7]

This passage from *Jesus Calling* was so powerful for me today. All manner of ideas just flooded my brain. Too many to capture actually. It is short and direct in its message. I read a story once about a man who lost two children in rapid succession. When his family came to comfort him, his reply was, "The Lord gave and the Lord as taken away; Blessed be the name of the Lord" (Job 1:21 NKJV). When I saw his response, my first thought, through tears, was, *Wow, do I have that much faith?* And my second thought was, *It feels kind of cold or harsh in some way.* I couldn't really put my finger on it. I tucked it away in my heart.

After losing John, this verse has surfaced many times in my readings, and I think I understand it a little better. When we are journeying through loss, we read this verse and tend to focus on, "the Lord taketh away." We are devastated by the loss we are enduring. But through a trust in the goodness and sovereignty of God, we can begin to be thankful that the Lord gave us that love in the first place. Without Him, I have nothing. I never have. That "cultivates a thankful heart" for me. Gratitude and a thankful heart aren't necessarily reflected to the world as laughter, sunshine, and daisies all the time. Sometimes a grateful attitude is most deeply demonstrated by trusting through tears. Blessed be the name of the Lord!

Personal Reflection

God is GOOD ~ ALL the time!

Journeying with Jesus

I was awakened with thoughts of thankfulness this morning.

Let me back up a bit. A few months ago, I presented my faith journey to our small group. At one point I remarked that I was always amazed to see how God has been working in my life, guiding my way, gently nudging me along. This was something I could see so clearly but always retrospectively, like the "Footprints in the Sand" image. During the past year, I feel like living a grateful life has really increased my connection with God. I have felt His presence through so many parts of my life—always in nature, always with family—but also often in conversations with complete strangers, in church or small groups, or whispers in the darkness.

I told our group that I have also recently discovered that I am a "Journey Christian." I am not sure if this is an actual thing—I just kind of made up the term—but it perfectly reflects that I am much less interested in the prosperity I will build up on earth, or even in heaven, than I am in walking every step of this life with Jesus. I pray each day to walk in bold humility—humility, knowing without a doubt that I am nothing without His grace, and boldly in the recognition that the Creator of the universe dwells within me. That part is really tough to get my arms around most of the time. The epiphany that I had this morning was that I know, right now, in this very present time, I am being carried. That Philippians 4:7 verse, "And the peace of God, which surpasses all understanding," I know *that peace.* So I woke up thankful this morning. Then I heard "Oceans," by Hillsong United, and blubbered a bit.

So I will call upon Your name
And keep my eyes above the waves
When oceans rise, my soul will rest in Your embrace
For I am Yours and You are mine.[8]

Message received! Smile!

Personal Reflection

God is GOOD ~ ALL the time!

Walking with Dad

It has been six months. I feel like I need to get a pack of those baby monthly milestone stickers you see on Facebook and wear the "6" for the day. This month we could celebrate the milestones: Six months and most nights she is sleeping through the night, she doesn't cry nearly as much, and, oh my, look how big she's gotten! Yes, my twisted sense of humor is slowly returning. That humor that made John laugh and occasionally declare, "Julie Renee!" when it went too far. The holidays are in the rear view, the boys have arrived safely at their respective destinations, the Clemson Tigers are national champs, and this woman decided to turn into a list-making, box-checking, road-running machine. As often happens when I am trying to achieve multiple mindless tasks, my brain shifts into overdrive. I think of millions of other little things that send me all over the house, and I never complete the first task! A couple days ago one of these little side excursions took me to a box that revealed a lot of memories. I discovered something I had forgotten was even in that box—John's high school journal. Since I was looking through the box for something specific, I just quickly flipped through the journal to remember what it was and from what time in John's life it had been written. However, something caught my eye, so I read the passage. John was seventeen when he wrote this:

> January 10, 1977 [Yes, exactly forty-two years ago, and no, I do not believe in coincidences.]

> It's on nights like these that the memories of May 13, 1972, flash into my mind. I won't ever forget my father, or how he lived and how he died. I remember when I was young, I used to get so disgusted because it always seemed that my older brother was better at everything than me. One night

we both spent our weekly allowances on model airplanes. I still remember seeing how crafty Mike's was while mine looked horrible. I remember how I got so disgusted that I threw mine on the floor and crushed it to pieces. I ran to Mom, but before I got to her, my father grabbed hold of me. I remember how afraid I was that he was going to punish me for my foolish deed, but to my surprise, my father asked me if I wanted to go for a walk with him. I agreed. It was particularly cold that night, but I didn't feel it as we walked all along the neighborhood streets. We talked, and through talking, my father calmed me and made me feel better.

I also remember a cold, rainy night in Ohio. My father had been in the hospital for a week now, and we were all afraid for him. He called us one night, and when it got to be my turn to speak to him, my voice cracked over the phone as tears filled my eyes. Never had I heard this great father of mine's voice sound so weak. I could hardly manage to make out what he said, but when I finally did, I could hold the tears back no longer, and I broke down and cried. "John," he said, "you sound like you should go for a walk." That was the last time I heard his voice. He died, but our last walk together had yet to come.

It was a brilliant, sunny day when the Mass was held at St Brendan's Church for the soul of my father. I was selected as a pallbearer for his casket. I was only thirteen, and I had an awful time carrying my father's body. My arm ached, yet I wanted to feel this pain for eternity. Tears streamed down my face, and I realized that this would be my father's and my last walk together. As I laid the casket down, I remembered how many times this man had carried my burdens, and how now I carried him to his final rest. I don't take walks anymore. I suppose it is because he isn't here to calm me. But I long for the day when we shall meet in heaven, and our walks shall be resumed for all time. "A man is never dead until he is forgotten." I will never let my father die.

Oh Lord, how I wept! I wept for the loss of my sweet guy. I wept for that young man who was so shaped by the loss of his father. I wept for my sons who must endure the same. But wrapped up in this blubberfest was a profound peace—"I long for the day when we shall meet in heaven." I felt like God was using John's past grief to reach through time to give his family fresh hope for a certain future.

This is really all about hope. My sons can see all that their dad achieved in life despite the loss he experienced. They saw how he lived, how he overcame, how he loved, the lessons he taught them on the walks they took. They can continue their paths while knowing that this is not the destination but merely a part of the journey to be continued. I am certain John is walking with his daddy, and this makes me smile.

Personal Reflection

God is GOOD ~ ALL the time!

Never Ending Love

Yesterday, somewhere in South Carolina, a young woman named Melissa said, "I do," to the love of her life. I couldn't help but think about her today when the gospel was read in church: Love is patient and kind; love does not envy or boast; it is not arrogant or rude. It does not insist on its own way; it is not irritable or resentful; it does not rejoice at wrongdoing, but rejoices with the truth. Love bears all things, believes all things, hopes all things, endures all things. Love never ends (1 Corinthians 13:4–8 ESV). I have never been to a wedding that didn't include this reading. Even our judge read it when John and I eloped to the Oktibbeha County Courthouse thirty years ago! Today, though, it was the last line that really hit me: "Love never ends."

You see, eight months ago, Melissa wasn't certain that her daddy would be able to walk her down the aisle or even be alive. This week I received a letter from the recipient of John's lungs: "Our youngest daughter, Melissa, is getting married March 2, 2019. She has chosen to honor your family, and in memory of John, place a single rose and an empty chair at the family table, for your choice to donate life and to allow her father to walk her down the aisle on her special day." That touched me in such a deeply profound way. Joy and pride and humility pushed away a little sadness. John's legacy of love just continues to ripple throughout this world, impacting lives upon lives in ways that we cannot imagine. Yes indeed, love never ends.

Personal Reflection

....

God is GOOD ~ ALL the time!

Nine Months

I think the perplexity of time is a commonly shared experience by people on this journey of grief. It seems as though it has already been such a long journey—nine months, 248 days, 5,952 hours, 357,120 minutes, 5 million breaths. There are times when it is just about taking that next breath. All that time, all those breaths, and yet, in the blink of an eye, I can be right back in that hospital room and feel as raw and desperate as I did on that day. I had a thought today that perhaps anniversary days seem more difficult because it is as if some invisible force turns your mind back to face that day, that moment forever frozen in time. I am grateful that most days are spent looking forward, trying to find my way on this new path, and thankful for the multitudes of memories that came before that day. Those memories bring such joy and comfort and gratitude.

I continue to trust that God has a plan much bigger than I can see. I do not pretend to understand His plan, or even agree with it for that matter. But I do believe in His sovereignty. I believe in His goodness. I believe in His love. I was having a little chat with God on the three-hour trip home today, and I might have mentioned that some affirmation regarding John would be nice, just a little smile from above. Perhaps a rainbow appearing in the cloudless sky or a llama standing by the road. Either of those would have made me squeal with delight! Well I was stopped at the last light before home, preparing to turn left, and a truck pulled up next to me. As I glanced to the right, I noticed a sticker on the driver's side window that said, "John Boy." As soon as I saw it, "I Can Only Imagine," by Mercy Me, came on the radio instantaneously. That song was played at the celebration of John's Life, and it always transports my thoughts to heaven and worship. Grin.

Personal Reflection

God is GOOD ~ ALL the time!

Psalm 46

God is our refuge and strength,
an ever-present help in trouble
Therefore we will not fear, though the earth give way
and the mountains fall into the heart of the sea,
though its waters roar and foam
and the mountains quake with their surging ...
He says, "Be still, and know that I am God."(Psalm 46:1–3, 10)

All week I have been hit with Psalm 46, either verses 1–3 or 10. I am reading a few books, have GriefShare homework, daily devotionals, and so on, and Psalm 46 has been in every single one of them. In fact, I am surprised there wasn't a billboard on the interstate this week that said, "Julie—Psalm 46— wink, wink." This gets me a little excited. Oh boy, oh boy! God is trying to tell me something, and I give a little happy wiggle. What is He trying to tell me? Am I meant to share this with someone else? Who? Is there a hidden meaning that I am missing? I talk to God about it. I ask for guidance or a clue. It just sits in the back of my head, ruminating.

Then while dragging in after a twelve-hour shift, thinking about a few of the million distractions that come with living each day in this fog called grief, it was clear as a bell. It was like God thumped me upside the head and said, "Sit down, be quiet, *listen*. I've got this!" I actually laughed! It turns out this has been the perfect verse for the week as I bumped into four people who had not yet heard about John. It is hard for me to fathom that the whole universe is not mourning with us. How could someone possibly not know? I imagine as I venture out of my cocoon more and more, this may occur more frequently. This first time, though, was awkward, tough. I think the hardest thing is seeing fresh grief in their eyes. It kind of opened my wounds a bit, and they felt fresh again. I didn't like it. But I held on to, "God is our refuge and strength, an ever-present help in trouble." It was right there in my brain. "Therefore, we will not fear *though the earth give way*" (emphasis added). That is exactly what it feels like sometimes. And then this morning I thought, *Silly, this verse is perfectly straightforward—and perfectly meant for you.* Then it washed over me: "Hush, precious child. I've got you." Sigh. Message received.

Personal Reflections

God is GOOD ~ ALL the time!

PART 2

· · · · · · · · · · · ·

Being Filled

The sun is rising blue and subdued this morning. I know it is out there somewhere, even if I cannot see it. Light is infusing the world; the seagulls have taken flight. Remember, just because you cannot see the Son or feel His warmth doesn't mean He isn't with you, filling you with His love, covering you with His grace.

For we live by believing and not by seeing. (2 Corinthians 5:7)

God is GOOD ~ ALL the time!

An Imperfect Vessel

After attending a spiritual retreat years ago, I told our priest that I felt so filled with the love of Christ and the Holy Spirit that if someone were to cut off my fingertips, light would explode in every direction. A little Holy Spirit laser show. For me, the Holy Trinity has always equated to love and light. When I read in *Jesus Calling* this morning about being created as imperfect, "earthen vessels designed to be filled with heavenly contents,"[9] I was reminded that all our cracks and damaged parts are just opportunities for light to shine into the world. During this time of the most extreme brokenness that I have ever experienced, my prayer has been for a continual filling—due to my excessive leaking—so that I might have the opportunity to share some light during my darkness. This has been a choice. This has been very intentional. And I often fail.

A couple days after John died, I had the most terrifying and vivid dream. We were driving in my van very fast—Daniel was driving, ahem—and there was a metal pole right in the middle of our lane. We hit it, and the van was violently ripped open. I was hurled into the atmosphere. I felt crushed under the pressure, like I couldn't breathe. But I could yell, and I was screaming for Jesus: "Jesus, I need You! Where are You? Please save me! Save this family!" I woke myself up screaming and gasping. It was such a realistic dream.

During the hardest times in life, I think we all have a choice. Do we cry out to Jesus, or do we allow ourselves to be pulled into the black hole of our sorrow? Each day, and often several times a day, I have to intentionally seek Him. Some days it still comes out as a searching scream as I wander on this journey. I am thankful for His grace and have never, not for one millisecond, regretted the choice to seek His light in my darkness. I still pray to show that light to the world.

This is the message we have heard from him and declare to you: God is light; in him there is no darkness at all. If we claim to have fellowship with him and yet walk in the darkness, we lie and do not live out the truth. (1 John 1:5–6 NLT)

Personal Reflection

God is GOOD ~ ALL the time!

Background Praise

I have a confession. This past week or so has been pretty tough. I blamed it on the situation. I blamed it on the holidays. I was just focused on getting through without too many memories getting churned up—as if that is possible. Having both of my sons home is such a blessing, but the sting of John's absence seems sharper somehow. It is kind of like when you do a jigsaw puzzle, and after putting together all the pieces, there is still a big chunk missing. You didn't realize it wasn't complete when the pieces were all scattered about. John's playfulness and laughter are potently absent. My world has seemed gray.

However, in my typical fashion, I was determined to attack this thing. I will power through each day. I will check things off my lists. I will fake it till I make it. But this has left me feeling hollow. I realized yesterday that I had, once again, picked up that burden of self-reliance and was pretty much telling God, "Back off, I got this!" Well, I don't. I never did. The beauty of it is that God has me, even when I am fighting His grip, giving perfunctory thanks, empty praises, half-hearted hallelujahs. It occurred to me that while I was going through the motions, I had lost my background praise. I am at my best and feel closest to God when I am fully present in the world, yet there is this soft background of praise in my brain, my heart. It can be a song or a verse or a prayer. It has been a gift. At any point I can switch my focus and get a little God hug. Well yesterday I realized it was gone when I was talking with a man and the background wasn't anything remotely uplifting, wise, or sympathetic. It was more like, "You gotta be kidding me. This guy looks like an old, dried-up piece of smoked beef jerky with a mouth that won't hush, spewing hate, reeking of gin and cigarettes. Yet he is still here, living, abusing his body, not giving a rip about anything. Really, God? Just so You know, this is enraging." Then not too long after that, and thanks to our PA with a new baby, the background was switched to, "The wheels on the bus go round and round, round and round." And it struck me that without God, we are kind of on that bus going round and round and round without any true destination.

I had to do a hard reboot. This journey of grief and faith is so intentional. It takes work to avoid the pit or the pity pot! I know when I seek God's wisdom in all circumstances, I feel like burdens are few, and joy is present. This morning I awoke to this verse of the day: "Call to me and I will answer you and tell you great and unsearchable things you do not know" (Jeremiah 33:3).

On my way to my appointments today, my world seemed bright again as I drove down the highway, noticing the beauty all around, and tearfully singing (yelling) this song in my typically off-key fashion:

> Make me empty
> So I can be filled
> 'Cause I'm still holding
> Onto my will
> And I'm completed
> When you are with me
> Make me empty. ("Keep Making Me," Sidewalk Prophets)[10]

Personal Reflection

God is GOOD ~ ALL the time!
(Even if We Forget Sometimes—That's Called Grace)

Barriers

God doesn't call the equipped; He equips the called. I have heard that saying for years. I don't know who first said it. I understood it at an intellectual level, but not at the gut level. For some reason, that is what I thought of when I read this in *Jesus Calling*: "You can live as close to Me as you choose. I set up no barriers between us; neither do I teardown barriers that you erect."[11]

The thing I have learned on this journey is that if you truly seek Him, He shows up. It suddenly explained the peace I had seen in others going through tough circumstances with so much grace. I would wonder, *How can she face that loss with such strength?* Or, *How could he possibly forgive the unforgivable?* The answer: Only with God's help. I have discovered a strength I could never have imagined, a peace, and so much love. However, first I needed to break down those barriers I had so expertly erected throughout the years, those barriers—pride, fear, self-reliance (my personal favorite), to name a few—that kept me from fully submitting and perfectly trusting. When the rubber met the road, God handed me a sledgehammer. Or better yet, one of those amazing shredding tools from Fortnite that demolish everything in their paths. My barriers fell in a heartbeat as I clawed my way to His arms because, "nothing in all creation will ever be able to separate us from the love of God that is revealed in Christ Jesus our Lord" (Romans 8:39 NLT).

Personal Reflection

God is GOOD ~ ALL the time!

Happy-ish New Year

After surviving Christmas, I have been looking forward to welcoming 2019 and putting 2018 behind me, behind us. The Grant family's absolutely, positively, most gut-wrenching year ever. But as each day marched toward the new year, I became more and more restless and edgy. It occurred to me this morning that while 2018 held some of the worst memories that I hold from this one life, it also holds some of the most precious ones, the last memories we ever made together. That last family vacation to Asheville, standing atop Mt. Mitchell, hiking in DuPont Forest, visiting the Biltmore and many of the microbreweries in that area. I smile remembering that John was not happy with us when we took the hike off-trail a bit, and how we all marveled that PB&J beer really tastes like peanut butter and jelly! Laughing until we cried at Aaron's Hunk videos, which he and Daniel were creating. Oh, how I miss that laughter. John and I spoke about how blessed we felt that our sons had become our friends, and we all still cherished our time together. It was that first "boys only" road trip to St. Louis that almost didn't happen. Those are memories the boys will hold dear, and probably embellish, forever. I am certain plans were made to have many more of those, albeit perhaps during a cooler month! It was many miles walked, side by side, conversing with my best friend, making plans, talking about our days, discussing so, so many things.

This morning those waves of grief pounded hard. Mixed with that grief, however, I am so blessed to always have hope. So as I got out of bed (yay, me!) and wiped away tears, I opened my devotional to this: "For I know the plans I have for you, declares the Lord, plans to prosper you and not to harm you, plans to give you hope and a future" (Jeremiah 29:11). As I look hopefully to the future, I am forever and always thankful for thirty-four years of wonderful, and 2018 will always be written on my heart.

Personal Reflection

....

God is GOOD ~ ALL the time!

Show-and-Tell

For ever since the world was created, people have seen the earth
and sky. Through everything God made, they can clearly see his
invisible qualities—his eternal power and divine nature. So they
have no excuse for not knowing God. (Romans 1:20 NLT)

I need to put this verse as the introduction to my gratitude journal. I am
blessed to see God so profoundly in nature. I actively hunt for His gifts
when I am outdoors; I seek His beauty. When you intentionally turn your
gaze from what has been lost to all that has been given, a shift occurs in
your spirit. I have found this to be one of the most helpful tools to draw on
while navigating the journey of grief. It is like a compass set outward. Over
the past couple years I have tried to become more intentional in not only
acknowledging the beauty that has been placed before me but also in giving
thanks for it. I think God loves it when we stop and just say, "Wow! Thank
you!" Whether it is for a beautiful sunset, an unexpected turn of providence,
or the comforts we may sometimes take for granted, I believe God wants to
be a part of our everyday worlds and goes to great lengths to draw us in! I
don't think He likes to play hide-and-seek nearly as much as He likes playing
show-and-tell!

Personal Reflection

God is GOOD ~ ALL the time!

The Burden of Love's Gift

Monday, December 19, 1988, was a clear, crisp, blue-sky day, much the same as today. It was on that day thirty-one years ago, in the Oktibbeha County Courthouse, in Starkville, Mississippi, that our judge pronounced John and me, husband and wife. The love affair that had begun over four years before became official. We were both graduating the following May, and we were very poor. In fact, the cottage we rented could literally fit into our current great room! We rolled the coins we had been saving and had enough for one night in a cabin at Lake Lowndes. Of course we also had to get back to Starkville because MSU was playing East Carolina in basketball at home the next night! I wouldn't change a thing. We never had a wedding, but we had a fantastic marriage. We didn't have much of a honeymoon, but we had some awesome adventures. We were like-minded on the things that mattered, and we compromised on the things that didn't. We had such a wonderful ride.

Oh, it wasn't perfect because we aren't perfect. But there was never a time that I wanted to be next to anyone else, not even for a second. It was a gift; we knew it was a blessing while we were living it. I read recently that in Hebrew, the root word for "gift" is the same as the root word for "burden." That makes perfect sense as the gift of love is always so delicately intertwined with the burden of loss. I looked this up to be sure; the word is *nasa*. I was struck to discover that it is also the root word for "uplifting," specifically the uplifting of hands in prayer. When returning the burden of the loss of love's gift back to the Giver, this is the only posture that will do.

Thanks be to God for his indescribable gift! (2 Corinthians 9:15)

Personal Reflection

God is GOOD ~ ALL the time!

God Goggles

While walking Pishwit around the lake this morning, I was listening to music and relishing the slight coolness of the breeze. I came upon a scene that stirred up so many emotions. There were three generations of men fishing off the retaining wall. Just as we walked by, the little boy, who was in the center of the three, turned to look at us. His little bobber bobbing from his beginner's pole, him grinning a large, squinty-eyed, toothless grin. I smiled even as I felt the tears welling up, spilling over. That was our dream standing right there in front of me, which was shattered in the blink of an eye. Our dreams were never of riches or extravagance. They were always of future family adventures, giving love and joy to the generations that would follow. I hadn't gone three steps when Lauren Daigle's words began: "Letting go of every single dream, I lay each one down at Your feet." I gave myself in to the music and listened, breathed it in, "I will trust, I will trust in You."[12] God definitely speaks to me through music and nature. Because I enjoy photography, I often see the world through a lens, either the lens of my camera or the one in my mind's eye. This was made obvious to me in a text exchange with Aaron a week or so ago.

> *Aaron:* I have realized no matter where you are, THERE'S ALWAYS SOMETHING TO BE SAD ABOUT. I don't think happiness is a lack of sadness. I think it's about choosing to look at what makes you happy.

> *Me:* I think you are exactly right. When you awaken grateful for each day and find joy in the smallest things, then you are blessed. It is all about learning what you choose to bring into sharp focus, what you leave blurred out in the

background, and what you decide to totally crop out of your view.

I believe that when God is the lens through which you see the world, it is so much easier to bring joy and love and hope into sharp focus. I pray for this each morning, that I see others as He does. You can call it kingdom eyes or the lens of grace, or even God goggles. No matter what you call it, the world looks better through it, and Him.

When I got home, Aaron and I cooked omelets and happy-danced to "Here Comes the Sun."

Personal Reflection

God is GOOD ~ ALL the time!

February

I pray that out of his glorious riches he may strengthen you with power through his Spirit in your inner being, so that Christ may dwell in your hearts through faith. And I pray that you, being rooted and established in love, may have power, together with all the Lord's holy people, to grasp how wide and long and high and deep is the love of Christ, and to know this love that surpasses knowledge—that you may be filled to the measure of all the fullness of God. (Ephesians 3:16–19)

This month has been a bit tough. On the tenth it was hard not to mark that it had been seven months since John's passing. That was followed in rapid succession by Valentine's Day and then his sixtieth birthday, all within about a week. So reading this today caused me to reflect on God's love—His amazing and humbling and, at times, overwhelming love. I remember exactly when I first had even a tiny grasp of how much He loves us. Daniel was about a week old; he was lying on my lap and stretching, and I was studying his perfect little post-feeding, milk coma, lip-puckered face. John was lying on the bed, and I turned to him and said, "You know, I love you more than I ever thought I could love someone. But this, this love I feel for him, this is something else. It is fierce. It is other-worldly. I would die for him. In a heartbeat." I thought that if I could love someone like that—me, a perfect example of an imperfect human—then I couldn't even fathom how much God loves us.

When I think about the sacrifice that Christ made for me, though, what He endured for me because of His great love, the humility can be almost crushing. I feel so unworthy. And yet I have felt Him reach through this current darkness and hold me close. In this I don't feel overwhelmed or crushed, only the greatest sense of peace. It just makes me want to shout, "His love is real! This peace is real!"

The way that I have found most helpful to stay tapped into this is to live a life steeped in gratitude, being thankful for every small way that God blesses me each and every day. Remember, God really is good all the time. Not just when life is all sunshine and bird-singing perfection, but even when, or maybe especially when, the path is dark and foggy and uncertain, and you don't know how you are going to get through. Ann Voskamp writes, "In Christ, you're a native of heaven right now. You aren't a citizen of here trying to work into heaven. You're a citizen of heaven trying to work through here."[13] That feels right to me because the times in my life when God's love just smacked me in the heart were the times when I was first in the presence of one so new from his Father in heaven and now when I long for one who is back home, enjoying the unfettered joy of God's love in his Father's presence.

Personal Reflection

God is GOOD ~ ALL the time!

Daddy's Boys

This morning was kind of gray inside and out. As I lay there thinking, praying, it occurred to me that I very much miss my baby-love, best friend, partner-in-crime, but the hardest has been saying goodbye to my boys' daddy. John totally rocked fatherhood! Oh, there are many stories of fatherhood (and motherhood) fails, but those just became fun tales of survival through the years. John was totally dedicated to his boys. I recently told someone who was pregnant that you love your husband as much as you think you possibly can, and then he becomes a daddy. That just opens a whole different place in your heart to love him. I fell in love with John all over again.

It always warmed my heart to hear them laughing, playing cards or games, or watching sports together. When they were little, there was always much giggling, and John was always making up games for them to play. As they grew older, the laughter was ever present, along with the trash talking.

I do believe, with all that I am, that this is part of a plan that is so much bigger than us, and we are really leaning on our faith and friends and prayers. As I have said many times, I love the Coach but hate the playbook right now. Church was a comfort and spoke to me today, a reminder to continue to praise Him in this storm. It also helped me get my daily hug quota.

Then I heard this song on the radio. Cue the floodgates:

Tell your heart to beat again
Close your eyes and breathe it in
Let the shadows fall away
Step into the light of grace
Yesterday's a closing door
And you don't live there anymore
So say goodbye to where you've been
And tell your heart to beat again.14
("Tell Your Heart to Beat Again," Danny Gokey)

Personal Reflection
....

God is GOOD ~ ALL the time!

My Song

I received a card yesterday, the day that marked eleven months. It was brightly colored with this Swedish proverb penned across the front:

Those who wish to sing, always find a song.

It made me smile. I love it! I thought, *This is nice. This is hopeful.* But as I read it again, it just reminds me that ultimately, how this journey goes depends on me, on the choices that I make. You see, first I must have the desire to sing, to live, to marvel at life's beauty. This is a conscious choice; it doesn't just happen as I passively exist. Then after desiring to sing, I will need to search actively for my new song. I cannot find without seeking.

Today I was asked how my faith has changed since John's death. I replied that it had strengthened significantly. And it has. But more than anything, my faith has gotten louder. I had always been kind of quiet about my faith, a bit timid to share it. But now? Not so much! So I know, without a doubt, my new song's chorus will reflect the faithfulness and grace and peace and joy that I have received during this time. And when I do find this new song, I will sing it loudly and boldly and pray that God is glorified by the singing.

Personal Reflection

God is GOOD ~ ALL the time!

Accepting the Present

I spent yesterday with John. His presence was all around as I was cleaning in my room and getting his things organized and put away. At some point the boys may question some of the choices I made regarding the items kept. It was hard for me to part with pictures that they had drawn through the years and John kept in his office. This touching of his things, this remembering, it felt like the right time. I was at peace.

After working most of the day, I went to Somerset Pointe on the lake with Pishwit, the jungle dog. That is another place where I feel so close to John. I was in a rather open area and just looking up at the clouds while the jungle dog intently smelled every blade of grass. Suddenly, out of nowhere, a large hawk soared overhead. He wasn't there, and then he was. So I smiled. God was winking. The hawk appeared and disappeared overhead during the entire one-mile loop. Since it was nearly time for the sun to set, I decided to try to watch the sun descend into the lake before returning home.

There was a big party of kids and families at the lakeside cabins. As I sat on the picnic table by our tree, the smell of woodsmoke wafted by on the breeze along with peals of laughter from the children as a massive game of hide-and-seek was about to ensue. Two pink-cheeked, excited faces ran toward me, and I swear it was Daniel and Aaron from years past.

As the game moved away from me, the mourning doves could be heard from the woods, along with the eagles who were returning to their nests for the night. I felt totally present in every aspect of that moment as I awaited the setting sun. In my silence, I did not grieve for future sunsets unseen but reveled in the multitude that had been shared. I breathed in the beauty and peace that were before me, accepting that gift with an open heart. Amid the cacophony, I sat alone but was not lonely, silent in the grace of His glory.

> Let the heavens rejoice, let the earth be glad; let the sea resound, and all that is in it. Let the fields be jubilant, and everything in them; let all the trees of the forest sing for joy. (Psalm 96:11–12)

Personal Reflection

God is GOOD ~ ALL the time!

Trust, Faith, Belief

Most people who know me know that I am a planner, a list-maker, a box-checker extraordinaire. John and I had many plans for our "Empty Nest—Take 2" situation that was approaching. Between that and upcoming retirements and big birthday trips, we had a nice five-year plan in the making. All those dreams were destroyed in a heartbeat when John was taken so suddenly and unexpectedly. Everything was silenced. Dreams, plans, hopes, expectations—gone. When I emerged from the rubble, I felt so lost. "What now, Lord?"

My faith had remained steadfast, but there were times when fear tried to slink in and whisper its lies. I knew in my heart that if the Lord had brought me to this place and totally obliterated my landscape, then certainly He must have a plan, a direction, a path—something. I wanted to know what He wanted me to do, where He wanted me to go, how He wanted me to glorify Him. I wanted to know everything and a new five-year plan revealed, preferably yesterday! I was walking so closely with Him, His Word illuminating each step, guiding me gently. Yet I wanted a super-strong LED light that you could see from space. I wanted to see far into the future, every direction simultaneously, not just the next step. He is so patient with me.

One night I prayed and prayed about this, a fervent, "What am I supposed to do with all this?" prayer. I fell asleep in prayer and dreamed I was walking along a busy highway. On the other side of the highway someone was trying to get my attention. It was a young man, waving and waving his arms over his head. I turned and looked, and he was standing under a huge black awning with equally large white letters that read, "2 Peter 3." Then I woke up! I was so excited! Lights on, Bible out, reading, reading, reading, and … hmmm? Brow-furrowing confusion. I was not sure what to do with that. I read that chapter over and over for days, trying to figure out what it had to do with me, with my walk. Then one day as I was rereading, the last verse struck me: "grow in the grace and knowledge of our Lord and Savior Jesus Christ. To him be the glory both now and to the day of eternity. Amen" (2 Peter 3:18 RSV).

It felt like God was telling me to trust Him, to continue to grow in my faith and knowledge of Him, and to walk this new path closely with Him. *Webster's Dictionary* defines "faith" as a firm belief in something for which there is no proof: complete trust.[15] That resonated with me. I have often said that faith and fear cannot coexist, but what I am learning on this journey is that belief and trust can *only* coexist. I am so thankful that I have placed both of those in the God who guides me, who teaches me, who carries me, who loves me.

Personal Reflection

God is GOOD ~ ALL the time!

Streams of Consciousness

I spoke to my sister today. That is always good. We often have a good laugh, usually about something silly that one of us has done. Today my face froze on her screen making a funny face, and she went into hysterics. It is always good just to vent to her. She is far away, so I don't feel like she thinks I expect her to attend to the items I am venting about. It frees me to rant. This week, for some reason, the loss of John in the everyday living of life has just been in my face. Like sitting on the toilet, looking at the empty roll, and knowing that no matter how loudly I yell, another will not magically appear on the end of an outstretched arm reaching through the bathroom door. Then there are the multitudes of tasks that are made so much more bearable when sharing them with someone as you chat about the day—like emptying the dishwasher. Ugh. There are those countless times when I think, *I wish I could tell that to John*, or worse yet, I reach for the phone to text him. I realized that missing our casual conversations had taken a scary turn when, after seeing a Women's History Month commercial on TV, I turned to Pishwit and asked if he knew about all the famous female dogs from history. Then I started trying to name them for him and realized there is a dearth of famous female dogs! I even googled this! They are all male dogs: Rin Tin Tin, Beethoven, Benji, Hooch. The list goes on, with the exception of Lassie, which, everyone knows, was predominantly played by male dogs. FYI: Pishwit was very attentive during this conversation.

Another thing I have noticed is that there are words that really get to me. For example, every time I see the word "wife" in writing or read about, "your role as a wife," I wince. It stings. I still feel like John's wife. I loved that role in my life. I wasn't ready not to be his wife. I still am not ready. That is made doubly apparent when filling out forms, and there have been a lot of forms. Sometimes the marital status question only offers two choices, single or married. I understand in my head that you are either one or the other, but I really get peeved when there isn't a "widowed" option. I take it as a personal affront. I give the form-presenter a squinty-eyed glare.

As I pondered these annoyances, it occurred to me that if there are waves of grief that can take you down to your knees or totally flatten you, then these things—these ever present "missings"—are the puddles you tromp through that can kind of keep you in a wet-footed, annoyed state. Well that thought just set off an entire cascade of imagery.

Since I am someone who enjoys walking, I always think of life as a journey. My journey, in my mind's eye, is a trail through the woods in the mountains, with times spent in valleys and times spent appreciating the views from the summit. Since losing John, there has been the appearance of a large lake of grief added to this imagery. Initially I thought I would drown in this lake created by our tears. But with the help of God and all my people on this journey with me, I am back on the trail. I have learned to give up my burdens. I have become more sure-footed and adept at navigating the puddles … usually. I have trusted when the way was dark and uncertain. I have learned to use the bridges built by faith and friendship to cross troubled water. I am not certain if the lake will grow smaller through time, but I feel that it will always be present in the center of my journey. For today, though, I will sit in the sunshine and let my feet dry in its warmth. I will look upon that lake and appreciate the beauty of the reflection of what once was. And I will be grateful.

> The Sovereign Lord is my strength; he makes my feet like
> the feet of a deer, he enables me to tread on the heights.
> (Habakkuk 3:19)

Personal Reflection

God is GOOD ~ ALL the time!

Seeing His Light

My online devotional yesterday was about maintaining an attitude of gratitude. Then I read this from Martha Whitmore Hickman's *Healing after Loss*: "One of the most healing things it is possible to do when one is experiencing profound grief is to try to isolate occasional wonderful moments from the stream of time."[16]

I have found that journaling my thankfulness each day has been my most life-changing habit. I had started this about a year before John died, and I felt that my walk with the Lord became so much sweeter, more intimate. I am optimistic by nature and consider myself to have a grateful spirit, but I had never been intentional about giving thanks to the Giver or actively seeking His points of light in my life. I was just aware of the beauty if I stumbled upon it. After losing John, when the landscape of my life became shadowed, I was so thankful for even the smallest points of light. And I was grateful that I had learned to see them, hold them, breathe them in, and give thanks.

> Rejoice always, pray continually, give thanks in all circumstances; for this is God's will for you in Christ Jesus. (1 Thessalonians 5:16–17)

Personal Reflection

God is GOOD ~ ALL the time!

The Second Year: You Don't Scare Me

It has been fourteen months without John. The last two-plus months have been a flurry of activity and emotion. There was a stress and edginess that I felt as the one-year mark approached. That coupled with household projects and travel have left me thankful for some downtime—or at least my normal level of busyness. Approaching the one-year mark was like being hurled toward darkness and uncertainty. I had read that many people mark this occasion in various ways and celebrations. Others talk about the second year being harder than the first. Gulp! That information didn't seem very helpful or hopeful. I knew that the boys and I were meeting in Greenville for Aaron to run a half-marathon in John's honor, but that was the extent of our plans. No big barbecue. No big party. I hoped John wouldn't be offended, but it just didn't feel right for us. Or maybe just for me.

I am not certain if my emotions were more apparent than I thought, but my coworkers, in their infinite caring and wisdom, covered a couple of my shifts, so I was able to have some time to myself in the mountains before meeting the boys. Just me, the jungle dog, and all my thoughts. I spent both days hiking in the DuPont Forest. We had gone there on our last family vacation, so as soon as my feet hit the trail, the memories flooded in. It occurred to me in my reminiscing that throughout this first year, my mind often goes back to what we were doing the previous year at the same time. But after you pass the first year, when you look back, the memories are of grief, grief in its freshness, raw grief. It's not that it has been a year since he died but that it has been a year since he lived, laughed, loved. That is what stabs.

Another thought I had was that many mark that year with the expectation they will be miraculously relieved of further grief or that life will return to a semblance of normal. I have never thought that. I am too pragmatic. But for those who do, when that sudden healing doesn't occur, I imagine it can be tough. To me, the second year kind of reveals the chronic nature of grief. For example, if you had a leg amputated, the first year is spent dealing with the pain, recovering, healing, learning to do the things you did before, and getting stronger. Then that second year rolls around, and you realize you still have a limp and the phantom pains that haunt your nights. I have seen healing; I have seen God working in my life. I have found an inner strength I never would have imagined. But a second doesn't go by that I do not know that I am forever changed by the loss of my sweet guy.

When I was in the mountains, I received the contact information for the recipient of John's lungs. Turns out they live right outside of Greenville. Of course they do! So exactly one year after saying goodbye to the love of my life, I was able to meet J. R., and the love of his life, Ann. The way God's timing worked in all of this was simply miraculous. I think being in the presence of those who were able to go on living, laughing, and loving because of John was absolutely the greatest way to celebrate his life and our love.

Personal Reflection

God is GOOD ~ ALL the time!

Shadows

I love to be outdoors and walking. I do some of my best thinking, problem-solving, singing, and praying while walking. St. Augustine called it *solvitur ambulando*: "It is solved by walking." I never knew it was an actual thing! Today was an absolutely glorious day to be outside. The sky was that perfect shade of deep, Carolina blue. The breeze was cool and the grass brilliant green. It was like walking in an ultra-HD world! As Pishwit and I were strolling along—it may have looked more like I was being pulled along as there were many fox squirrels scurrying about—shadows crossed my path. I always love when I notice shadows darting across my path while I am walking. I stop and look up, hopeful to get a glimpse of the shadow maker. I have seen bald eagles soaring, ospreys carrying fish in their talons, and butterflies whose wings appear like stained glass as they silently drift above. It is so cool because this beauty was overhead all along, but I never would have noticed it without the shadow. Today I realized that the shadows we encounter in life are maybe meant to cause us to stop, look up, and see what beauty God has in store for us.

On the way home, Pishwit and I listened to "Somewhere Over the Rainbow," the Israel Kamakawiwo'ole version, with the windows down and sun shining in.

Personal Reflection

....

God is GOOD ~ ALL the time!

Mountains

We have just returned from a semi-technology-free trip to the mountains. Thanks to my friend Carol for the use of her family's cabin in the woods! We stopped in Clemson to scatter some of John's ashes and enjoy all the places he loved. John watched Clemson football *reruns* regularly. Nothing could turn around a bad day for John Grant like watching Clemson defeat Alabama for the Natty! I actually think we own that game!

Then we headed to the cabin in Bryson City, and God started winking like crazy. We took Pishwit, the ferocious jungle dog, who did awesome with traveling BTW. I was preparing to put him outside on a lead when he put on the brakes and was totally focused. I looked out, and right off the porch was the biggest elk that I have ever been that close to—like thirty feet away. I tiptoed like a cartoon character to get my camera and whisper/holler to the boys. We watched the elk wander around the yard and go off to the woods. I ran into one of the neighbors and mentioned my sighting. He looked at me like I was a naive city girl and said he had been there thirty years and had never seen an elk. Well, she made two more trips through that afternoon. Then the wind chimes on the porch gave a little tinkle; there was no wind. We smiled. I really felt John's presence with me so much in the mountains, maybe because there is no tech service or maybe because that is a place we loved. God always winked at both of us there.

I spent the next day with Daniel and Aaron, walking around the Nantahala Outdoor Center. I got hit by one of those big waves of melancholy when I let John's ashes go over his favorite rapid, the one he always managed to get turned around on and go down backward! I don't know if it was so much sadness in that moment as it was the acknowledgment of the loss of future joy with my life's companion. Even with that blip, the trip was another step on our journey of healing. I read this when I returned home: "In a broken world—when we remember how He blesses, loves us, when we recollect His goodnesses to us, we heal—we re-member" (Ann Voskamp).[17]

I like that, re-member, putting ourselves back together again, with God's help.

Personal Reflection

God is GOOD ~ ALL the time!

Being Held

I had a health concern recently. It wasn't something totally new to me because for years after my annual mammograms, I always had to get ultrasounds or additional views. But this year the doctor said we needed to do a biopsy. That word stopped me in my tracks. When you lose your spouse, father of your children, the fact that you are the surviving parent is never far from your thoughts. Who will love and console and encourage and love and support and guide and, did I say love my sons with the same ferocity I do if something happens to me? So for about a day, I was kind of stressing out a bit. Then I did what I tell everyone I know to do with their burdens: I laid it at the foot of the cross. It provided me with a measure of peace. A few days later I told some of my prayer warrior friends as well.

On the morning of the procedure, as I was driving to the hospital, I felt "held." It was beyond peace. It was as if I had been placed squarely in the arms of a very loving Savior. I was not nervous or worried or apprehensive about any of it. This was kind of an epiphany for me. When we lay our burdens at Christ's feet, we give them up for Him to take care of. When we ask for prayer or lift others in prayer, it is then that we place them in the arms of a very loving God.

As I prepared for my procedure, I received a message from a friend who had just returned from the funeral of her dear friend's husband. He had died unexpectedly. That hits home every time. I know that place. As I waited in that dressing room in that silly little gown, I sat down and turned my gaze outward, away from any of my concerns, and lifted that family in prayer. I prayed that they would land squarely in the arms of Jesus.

And because God's timing is perfect, this is the song that was playing when I left my procedure (which all turned out to be fine, BTW).

> So when you're on your knees and answers seem so far away
> You're not alone, stop holding on and just be held
> Your world's not falling apart, it's falling into place
> I'm on the throne, stop holding on and just be held.[18]
> ("Just be Held," Casting Crowns)

Personal Reflection

God is GOOD ~ ALL the time!

Dusty Roads and Rubber Boots

I got a pedicure recently. A young husband and wife work in the place where I go. He is big, has these happy eyes, and is always laughing and joking. She tries so hard to be serious. This last visit he was especially full of himself— nonstop talking and laughing, like really belly laughing. She would give him the side-eye, take a breath, and shake her head. Occasionally she said something to him in Vietnamese with a false bravado. Oh, he knew he was getting to her. He kept on. Then that long-awaited moment. Since she was facing me, I saw it first. The corner of her mouth was turning up ever so slightly. Then laughter danced everywhere. The whole place erupted. She acted mad that he had succeeded, but the smile settled in her eyes.

What a blessing to be able to work with your best friend. It can be challenging as well. John and I met and started dating while we were in training in the Peace Corps in Ecuador in 1984. When we were placed at our permanent sites, I was an aquaculture extensionist in a large rural area in the jungle, and John was in the provincial capital, fifteen miles away. He worked in the Ministry of Agriculture office and had a fish station where we grew mirror carp and tilapia. Mirror carp fingerlings were in high demand by my farmers. They grow big and quickly, but they are very difficult to reproduce, unlike tilapia, which I am convinced can reproduce on dry land. So our goal was to pull off a successful carp reproduction, which had never been accomplished successfully in that area. John liked to think he was my boss; I did not share this view! I won't go into great detail, but this is an extremely labor-intensive process that involves tricking the carp at every level to make them think it is the flood season in China and that they are ready to reproduce in the rice fields. It takes weeks of harvesting, checking fish, pond preparation, and then followed by more harvesting and more checking. I would stay at John's site during this time. The station was three miles from town, and we walked there every morning, back to town for siesta, back to the station in the afternoon, and back in the evening. Sometimes, if we were lucky, we would get picked up by a passing truck. We had a lot of opportunities to get to know each other well during three hours of walking each day. We laughed and talked and shared dreams and aspirations and beliefs. We fell in love on dirt roads in rubber boots, side by side. But there were some bumps along the way.

Our first attempt at carp reproduction yielded a very small success. But our second was the most successful reproduction ever in the history of aquaculture in Ecuador at that time. We produced close to six thousand fingerlings, more than adequate for the local farmers. John was determined that every single one of them would survive. We started going out to the station on the weekends. When he became especially dictatorial, I called him "King Carp" and gave him a little curtsy. He was not amused. During those twelve miles of walking each day, we had some huge arguments about how to raise carp fingerlings properly. In fact, we fought so much, we decided that when we got back to the States, we would take things slowly with regard to our relationship. It turns out that the proper raising of carp fingerlings is about the only thing we didn't agree on. Thank You, Jesus! We didn't even argue as much about raising kids!

I love these little strolls down the dusty roads of memory lane. They make my heart smile. And this one popped up all because my toenails were looking gnarly.

Personal Reflection

God is GOOD ~ ALL the time!

I Wish

It was such a long shift in the ER. I was dead dog tired. One of those twelve-hour days spent running nonstop from room to room and down the halls. I was absolutely beat. I came home, walked the dog, ate a quick meal, and then settled in for some downtime and the evening Pishwit snuggle ritual. I clicked on the TV and the app screen appeared. I was fiddling with the remote, looking for Netflix, and then I saw it. I just stared. Right there on the YouTube app was written, "I wish I could lay down beside you when the day is done." That was it, just those words. I smiled wistfully and said aloud, "So do I, baby. So do I." That was the perfect Godwink for the most imperfect day. I am such a spoiled child of God.

Personal Reflection

God is GOOD ~ ALL the time!

PART 3

· · · · · · · · · · · ·

Being Poured Out

With springtime, comes hope.
This feels true.
I laughed the other day.
I laughed until I couldn't catch my breath, and
tears were streaming down my face.
It felt so good.
Then memories of many such laughs from the
past poured into my consciousness.
I was thankful.

God is GOOD ~ ALL the time!

The Strength of Letting Go

As a GriefShare facilitator, I have often advised people that there are things that cannot be fixed and answers that will never be found. And as such, they just need to be left at the foot of the cross. What else can we do with unresolved regrets after the object of that regret has died? What about the apology that will never be received or all the unanswered whys that can turn the loss of a loved one into a life crippled by the never-ending struggle to understand what is outside one's grasp? These things can critically inhibit the ability to process not only grief but life as well.

Releasing burdens to the One who promises to carry them should be so easy. Just drop them and walk away, knowing the Creator of the universe can probably handle it. Why is it so hard to leave our burdens there? It occurred to me that maybe it is because it's not a matter of just letting go, as you would drop a load of wood that has become too heavy to carry. The dropping in that situation would bring relief. Maybe it is because we are buried under and entangled in the most precious burdens we bear. It is not a matter of simply dropping them but of getting out from under their weight, of disentangling ourselves from them. It is a matter of remembering what is within our power to control and what is not.

I have found that relief is waiting. All we have to do is ask the Lord to take that burden from us, release us from it. The irony is that it takes such strength to let go—strength of faith, the strength to trust. It takes strength to take that first step away from that which has smothered and bound us, and to take a step toward the life that God has waiting. Psalm 28:7 gives us hope: "The Lord is my strength and shield. I trust Him with all my heart. He helps me, and my heart is filled with joy. I burst out in songs of thanksgiving."

What is stopping you? Ask. You might have to ask more than once. Not because God doesn't hear you but because the strings that bind you to that burden can be plentiful or hidden. Or worse yet, like bungee cords, the whole thing pops back at you as you try to free yourself. Keep the faith, though! There is nothing like moving forward with a lightened load, a lifted heart, singing praises to the God who created you for worship, loves you as His child, and promises to set you free.

> Come to me, all you who are weary and burdened, and I will give you rest. (Matthew 11:28)

Personal Reflection

God is GOOD ~ ALL the time!

Grief Marathons

Facebook reminded me that it was six years ago, on January 20, that I ran the Charleston Marathon. Afterwards, I announced that I was no longer a marathon virgin, but I feared it would be a one-night stand. The actual marathon wasn't so bad; it was the training that was all consuming. I couldn't skimp on the training, or I would have never made it to the end. (Many wondered if I would make it to the end *with* the training!) I did my long runs during the week on my day off. I remember John asking what I had done one day, and I was like, "Well, I ran for four hours and then did a load of laundry. Yep, that's about it." It was so consuming.

I feel grieving is a little bit like that. There are things you just have to get through in order to get to the other side of it. Grief cannot be ignored or escaped; you must face it, battle it, yell at it, and find a way to make peace with it. God has showed up big time for me in this process. His Word has never been more relevant to me. He has kept His promises and shown me true peace. I cannot imagine walking without Him by my side, even if I do give Him the side-eye at times! We have been showered with prayers and love and hugs and support of every kind, and it strengthens us. There are lonely times. Not that "Let's go to lunch," kind of loneliness, but the, "Deep hole in my heart, my soul," kind. And paradoxically, it is best filled by being alone, filling that hole with memories of love and joy and laughter and tears. I can immerse myself, face them, love them, and fold them neatly into my heart. That has been my process over the past couple of weeks.

I am grateful for every memory, and I am thankful that we were able to come to this place without the burden of regret. What a blessing that is! Do we wish we had more time? Absolutely! Did our family do our best to love each other well each and every day for the time we had? Yes! That brings such peace.

Family is precious. Your spouse is that person you choose to do life with. Your children are products of that love. Don't play mind games or hold your love for ransom; it is never worth it. Love each other well. Be kind. Find joy. You will never regret it. And on the practical side, draw up a will, be sure beneficiaries are updated, make sure the non-bill-paying spouse knows about all the accounts, passwords, and so on. Do whatever you can to make sure the process will run smoothly in the event of an untimely death. Talk to each other about your wishes.

I think that working in the ER has made me very aware that death comes for everyone, and it is not necessarily planned or pretty. John and I had conversations about what if? That was such a blessing because I knew John's wishes. All the logistics were seamless. Having all these things sorted allowed me to focus on Daniel and Aaron and our grief. I was turning all of this over in my head this morning on my way to work, and "The Well" by Casting Crowns came on the radio.

> So bring me your heart, no matter how broken,
> Just come as you are, when your last prayer is spoken,
> Just rest in my arms a while, you'll feel the change my child,
> When you come to the well.[19]

Personal Reflection

God is GOOD ~ ALL the time!

The Gift

Blessed are those who mourn, for they will be comforted.(Matthew 5:4)

Over the past eighteen months I have encountered this verse frequently in my daily study and processing the loss of John. I haven't found mourning to be comfortable, but I have found it to be necessary. It is an emptying of self with guttural groans that emanate from the deepest part of the heart, the soul. And once emptied, there in the darkness, all alone, is where I found the gift. This gift has been there since Creation but gets so obscured and jostled and pushed aside by life and love and busyness that it is often overlooked. Even the many blessings we have been given can cloud our views of it. This gift is the Spirit of God wrapped tenderly in His Word. I have found it speaks to our hearts most clearly in the darkness.

Discovering God through His Word is new to me. I have had to be intentional. I am naive in my interpretations and my knowledge. I get excited by things I read that apparently are new only to me. My eyes sometimes cross while I am reading about every person from Adam to Abraham in 1 Chronicles. But I am determined because God has spoken to me so clearly through His Word during this time in my life.

So as I was processing all these thoughts in a flurry of study this morning, I read this in John Eldredge's *Restoration Year*, "Sometimes the sorrows of your life are in part God's weaning process. We give our hearts over to so many things other than God because we look to so many other things for life."[20] Exactly! What he said! A weaning process! This really struck me partly because when you lose someone who is so central to your being, the natural inclination is to hold everything else you love even more tightly. But in doing so, God can be obscured. Idols may be created. In the letting go,

I have found peace. In this mortal loss I have found a fullness of spirit, the most brilliant light in the darkest night. I have seen the beauty from ashes. I have discovered hope. Hope in His Word, comfort in the promises therein, and a strength that lies in trusting the God of the universe, who sits on the throne of my heart. Keeping Him there, unencumbered by my life, is a daily struggle, but I know this:

> I can do everything through Christ who gives
> me strength. (Philippians 4:13 NLT)

Personal Reflection
....

God is GOOD ~ ALL the time!

Prairie Dogs and Sunflowers

This excerpt from Sarah Young's *Jesus Calling* really spoke to me today, "Grow strong in the Light of My Presence. As My Face shines upon you, you receive nutrients that enhance your growth in grace."[21] When we were in Colorado, one sunrise was spent on a wildlife preserve. I marveled at the way the prairie dogs (Squeal! Happy wiggles!) were standing together, all turned toward the sun. And while visiting the botanical gardens, all the sunflowers also turned to the light. I have felt the light of His presence giving me strength over the past year but especially since John's passing, as I have more intentionally sought the Son. I have felt His light through the prayers of friends and family. I have felt it through cards and hugs and calls and music and invitations for fellowship. I have even felt it through the encouragement of strangers who have read my posts! Isn't that how it is supposed to be? Aren't we supposed to reflect the light of Christ in this world through our acts, words, and deeds? I love the line in Jason Gray's song, "With Every Act of Love," that says:

> God put a million, million doors in the world
> For His love to walk through
> One of those doors is you.[22]

The image of my being a door for God's love to pass through brings me immense joy. I find the more I study and the more grateful I am for all that I have, the less I feel sad about what I have lost. That does not mean feelings don't arrive, uninvited, into my day. It does mean that I have a safe place to turn to be nourished and grow in grace.

Personal Reflection

God is GOOD ~ ALL the time!

Musings of a Day of Errand Running

When I was walking into Walmart today, the memory of the boys and my first trip out after John died popped into my head. It was probably about a week afterward. We were clustered together, making our way into the same store. We talked about how weird it felt to be doing something so normal when our world still felt like it was falling apart. I remember saying that it seemed weird that everyone around us, bustling here and there, was completely oblivious to what we were going through. I felt like I needed to have a flashing neon sign over my head that said, "Broken—Handle Carefully." Almost simultaneously, though, I had the thought that we probably weren't the only people going through something so serious, so devastating. Some people might even have been going through something much worse. They needed their own flashing signs. When you really look at people, their struggles are sometimes right there for all to see. At other times, they are expertly hidden. I think that is why we should always choose to respond with kindness. We just never really understand what is going on in someone's world.

Perhaps God gave me this flashback because I was really struggling with "Judgey Julie" yesterday at work. My thoughts were something like, *So why did you think that bringing your entire family of six to the ER for sore throats was an appropriate use of time and resources?* And then, *So what exactly made this shoulder pain you've had for a year and toe pain you've had for six months suddenly an emergency today?* Of course these were said with raised eyebrows and my best are-you-kidding-me look. So I prayed for God to give me His eyes.

When I got home from shopping, I was determined that today I would go through one of John's boxes. It has been on the to-do list for weeks, and it is so far a to-didn't. Today I am going to do it. So I opened the box, and right on top was a sticky note, "Proverbs 18:13," written in John's hand. "Oh, this is going to be good," I mused. I closed the box and went to the Bible: "He who answers before listening—that is his folly and his shame." Well how often do I do that? I think we are all guilty of formulating our responses instead of really listening to what is being said. I know that by intentionally listening to someone, I am better able to understand his or her point of view. I may even change my opinion. I might actually grow a little as a human being. That understanding really makes it less likely that I revert to Judgey Julie. So now I guess I have to pray for God's eyes *and* His ears. I will do just that right before I open that box again!

> If you judge people, you have no time to love them. (Mother Teresa)

Personal Reflection

God is GOOD ~ ALL the time!

Light Ripples

Last night I spoke on the phone with the young lady who received John's left kidney. We were both a little nervous. We have exchanged texts and cards but have never spoken. She was so excited to finally speak because she just wasn't sure the cards and texts had adequately conveyed just how grateful she was for the gift of life. Her excitement was palpable even though she was trying to restrain herself. She spoke about how humbling it is and how our loss is not lost on her. She is so careful not to step on toes or push too hard. She wanted Daniel, Aaron, and I to know that she thinks about us and prays for us daily. She kept talking with her mother, who was present, while she was talking to me. Finally, she gave up and gave the phone to her mom, who was tearful and so very thankful. Her mother told me how wonderful it was to see her daughter doing so well and be so full of life. They were both so joyful and joy-filled it made my heart smile. She said all her very large extended family have become organ donors because of this. John is smiling, I am sure.

After the conversation I had the thought that when you lose someone, it makes your world dimmer, especially when that person's light had shone so brightly before. But when that person was able to donate a part of himself to others, his light is still able to burn brightly through that person or persons, and the whole world becomes a bit brighter. A little Romans 8:28 in action: "And we know that in all things God works for the good of those who love him."

Personal Reflection

God is GOOD ~ ALL the time!

Skydiving

On the morning of our most recent Loss of a Spouse class with GriefShare, I read a commentary about grief as it pertains to the loss of a loved one after an extended illness. One thought is that people already grieve during the illness, so the grief may not be as overwhelming after the actual loss. The commentator replied something to the effect that this was like saying you could experience skydiving while still sitting in the plane. That resonated with me because until you jump out of the plane, it isn't real. Until you say goodbye, it isn't real. I have thought a lot about this analogy. I think when a loved one receives a terminal diagnosis, you are forced to board a skydiving plane. You are grippingly aware of the journey that you are on. In some part of your consciousness, you are preparing yourself, checking flight plans, looking at landing sites, and meticulously packing the parachute you hope you will never have to use. You probably think you have it all together until the bottom drops out of the plane, and you are hurled into a Cat 5 hurricane. It is then that you realize you weren't prepared nearly well enough. But you have your chute, and you have been running through the scenarios. So in a way, maybe you are better equipped to navigate the journey ahead than those who experience sudden loss.

For those of us who have experienced sudden loss, we are just happily flying along, thinking we are headed to Disney World. Then suddenly, the bottom of the plane disappears, and we are hurled into that same Cat 5 hurricane. At some point someone throws a parachute out of the plane.

I started thinking that maybe our faith is represented by that parachute. Most of the people I have known who received a life-altering diagnosis quickly turned toward their faith and to God. They tended to their faith carefully during the illness and clung to it desperately if the battle was lost.

As for me, I had been growing stronger in my faith before John died so abruptly. My faith journey had been intentional and significant. Even in the hospital I felt that God had been preparing me for that time and fitting me for the parachute that I didn't even know I would need. When I was hurled out of the plane, I was thankful that my parachute was so close at hand.

Where is your parachute?

Personal Reflection

God is GOOD ~ ALL the time!

Listening

I am always excited to have my chicks under my wings. I was so looking forward to the opportunity we had to gather in Colorado for a few days. These gatherings are also mixed with a little anxiety. As I have said before, you can't fully appreciate the missing pieces of a jigsaw puzzle until you put it together, and our gatherings always exposes that gaping hole right through the heart of our family. The boys and I have discussed it. We recognize that we are still finding our ways on this journey, so we give each other a bit of grace for the edginess that is apparent.

Hiking in the mountains reminded me in many ways of this journey of grief that we have been on. On our first hike to a 10,000-foot peak, there were times that I became a little breathless. It was helpful to stop and shift my focus to the beauty that was all around and just breathe. I have found this tactic helpful on this journey of grief as well. Look outward, look upward, and just breathe.

It snowed that night, and the next day the trail was icy and uncertain. It was a little intimidating at first. We had to regroup back at the car, gathering the tools we had—one pair of snow grippers and three walking sticks—before beginning. There was a lot of debate about whether we should even begin. In the end we decided to just go, one step at a time, until we either reached our destination or couldn't go any further. Life feels that way sometimes, but taking that first step is so important. And then the next, and then the next. We made it all the way to Emerald Lake one slippery step at a time! I came away from this adventure refreshed and exhilarated.

The boys and I are finding our ways. While John's absence is even more gaping when we are together, I did notice something this time that hadn't been apparent to me before: I could hear John's voice most clearly when we were all together. We have always been the Grant family pod, spending so much time together that we all knew what John would have said or done in just about every situation. And we talked about it. He would have loved the Mexican and Indian restaurants; he would have been so irritated that the Cardinals let the Braves come back and beat them in the ninth; he would have loved the wildlife and the vistas and the beauty. On that last snowy hike, however, I think we all heard him say very loudly, "This is *not* a good idea!"

I had to jump back into life immediately on my return from Colorado. I am continuing to journey on, however, looking for beauty hidden and thankful for John's voice on the wind.

Personal Reflection

God is GOOD ~ ALL the time!

Equipped

I can do all things through Christ, who gives me
strength. (Philippians 4:13 NKJV)

I have recited this verse for many years and in so many situations, from training for a marathon, to giving a talk in front of a room full of people, to surviving the loss of John. It doesn't mean that God is going to miraculously lift you out of your circumstance, or that you are going to receive superpowers to accomplish some athletic feat. No. It means Christ is going to be walking beside you through whatever challenge you are facing, equipping you along the way. It means facing life with the peace that comes with knowing you are held, and then letting go and letting Him.

Personal Reflection

God is GOOD ~ ALL the time!

Encounters

Really, there is nothing you can say that will make their loss hurt less. It's going to hurt for a while. They're not looking to you to make sense of it or to say something they haven't thought of or something that makes it not hurt. Your purpose in saying something is to enter into the hurt with them and let them know they are not alone.
—Nancy Guthrie, *What Grieving People Wish You Knew*

I can relate to this passage. I feel certain it happens fairly regularly with everyone who has lost a loved one. I have run into people I haven't seen in a while who knew John and me casually from sports or raising kids or living in a small town. Their initial reactions on seeing me are a wave and a smile. Then, and you can almost see the realization register on their faces, "Oh, that's right." Suddenly their whole countenances change. It is always a bit awkward. I stumble all over my words, trying to put them at ease. It seems as though they would like to be anywhere else! In the last couple weeks I have been able to see some of John's coworkers in passing or at the recent mosquito control meeting. These encounters have been much different, but if you think about it, it makes perfect sense.

About a third of our daily lives are spent in the company of strangers who come together in this thing called work. If you are lucky, these strangers become your friends, and through time and shared experiences, they become your work family. What a blessing that is. My work family has loved me so well during this time. They have worked my shifts, fed our family, and prayed for us. They continue to give me a bit of space when I am quiet. They recognize my grief, but their grief is due to sadness for me and the boys, not because they feel the loss of John directly. He wasn't a part of their lives except through Daniel, Aaron, and me. Work is a kind of haven for me. My work "peeps" pretty much interact with me the same and don't look at me with the sting of loss in their eyes.

John was equally blessed, and he truly loved his work family. When I see them, I really sense our shared grief. But there is a hesitance on their parts to reveal it to me, maybe for fear of offending me or hurting me in some way. Maybe they feel that their grief couldn't possibly measure up to mine. Or maybe they just don't want to open that wound. Well let me tell you, if it takes a village to raise a child, then it certainly takes one to mourn a loss. I say this to open the door and let those who loved John know that I am okay with sharing this burden with you. In fact, doing so may make the load lighter. Unfortunately, I do not hold every memory of John that exists. I wish I did. But you, his work family and even lifelong friends, possess many memories. You saw John when he was happy and grumpy and proud and goofy. Perhaps the Robot wasn't always his dance move of choice! This is important information. I would welcome any opportunity to share those memories. I believe that holds true for anyone who has experienced the loss of a loved one. Anytime you feel like sending a text or a message or sharing a meal, please don't hesitate. Our eyes might fill, and tears might fall, but what if we laugh?

Personal Reflection

God is GOOD ~ ALL the time!

Connected Hearts

A picture memory popped up in my Facebook feed today. It is a picture of John's and my wedding rings laying one over the other down the spine of the open Bible. And when you get the lighting right, you can see that our rings form two heart-shaped shadows that are connected. It always gives me a wistful smile. I tried to capture the shot, flashlights precariously aimed in order to create the perfect image, this image of our hearts' connection through the covenant of gold rings.

I remember that John was watching football nearby in the living room, looking at baseball cards on his phone, and I was trying to find which Bible would display the rings, as well as the Bible verse, the way it was created in my mind's eye. This was during the season we were learning to enjoy our empty nest; Daniel was in Belize, and Aaron was at Clemson. Oh, we rocked that empty nest.

Such a comfortable love we shared. My heart is forever connected with John's. That knowledge brings more comfort than sadness. Henri Nouwen describes remembered love as a, "living force which sustains us in the present." Carrying our love with me and absorbing it into who I am becoming have been foundational for me on this journey.

> And now these three remain: Faith, hope and love. But the
> greatest of these is love.
> (1 Corinthians 13:13)

Personal Reflection

God is GOOD ~ ALL the time!

Sunrays and Moonbeams

Watching as darkness gives way to light over the Atlantic always fills me with joy … and hope. A new day with unfettered potential awaiting. Whether the sunrise is subdued and calming or spectacularly glorious, it elicits an audible sigh. The colors change, and the birds start calling and taking flight even before the first sliver of light appears over the horizon. I watch in anticipation for that moment when the sun gets just high enough to send a sunbeam across the ocean and straight to my feet. Isn't it cool that every person who has ventured out to watch the world wake up, no matter where they are on the beach, encounters that same gift? A sunbeam set at their feet. I wonder if they have ever had that same thought. Did they even notice the gift? I still feel that it is a gift just for me. I am thankful and thanks-filled.

I often think the beauty I encounter in this life has been placed specifically for my personal enjoyment. I really haven't changed much in this regard. I am reminded of a time when I was very small. We were driving through the mountains at night, and I was in that perfect place for safe mountain riding, lying on the ledge over the backseat, looking out through the rear window. The road was winding, and the moon was so bright that night. No matter how many hairpin turns we navigated, the moon was still there. Finally, I declared, "This crazy moon is following us everywhere through the mountains." Clearly, it was placed in the sky just for me. When someone later told me that the moon doesn't make its own light but merely reflects the light of the sun, I thought that was a pretty cool revelation.

I often pray to be a moon in the world, reflecting the light of the Son. It is my goal on most days, and on most days I fall short. However, a new day is coming, so I will journey on with a Son-beam set at my feet!

Blessed are those who have learned to acclaim you, who walk in the light of your presence, O Lord. They rejoice in your name all day long; they exult in your righteousness. (Psalm 89:15–16)

Here's another way to put it: You're here to be light, bringing out the God-colors in the world. God is not a secret to be kept. We're going public with this, as public as a city on a hill. If I make you light-bearers, you don't think I'm going to hide you under a bucket, do you? I'm putting you on a light stand. Now that I've put you there on a hilltop, on a light stand—Shine! (Matthew 5:14 MSG)

Personal Reflection

God is GOOD ~ ALL the time!

Someone Worth Dying For

A couple weeks ago I was listening to the song "Someone Worth Dying For," singing along while mindlessly folding laundry. As I was singing the ending—

> You're not just some wandering soul
> That can't be seen and can't be known
> You gotta believe, you gotta believe
> That you are someone worth dying for[23]

—the words kind of stuck in my throat. I sing these words, but do I really feel that way? Am I someone worth dying for? Do I live that way? When I saw the movie *The Passion of Christ*, I was so overwhelmed by humility and guilt and sadness. I felt so unworthy to receive the gift of God's grace, so broken, so flawed. When I look at the plain cross above the altar in our sanctuary, there are times I have to look away. I can't bear it.

As I was mulling this over while matching socks and stacking towels, a thought about my sons occurred to me. I know that I would lay down my life for them. It's not even a question. They aren't perfect, but that doesn't matter to me. Their worthiness is totally irrelevant. They are my sons; I love them. And then I had the aha moment: It's not so much that I live like I am someone worth dying for, it is more important that I live like a child of God. The love I have for my sons doesn't even begin to compare to how much I am loved by our Creator. All of us are—the good, the bad, and the ugly. Our value is found in His love, not because we are worthy, but because we are loved. God proclaims His love throughout the Bible. We just need to learn to trust that it is truth. You are a child of God. You are wonderfully made, dearly loved and precious in His sight (Psalm 139, paraphrased).

God is GOOD ~ ALL the time!

Answered Prayers

I absolutely believe in the power of prayer. I have received instant answers to prayers lifted and have been the beneficiary of the comfort and peace that come from being lifted in prayer. A week doesn't go by that I don't receive a request for prayer from friends or acquaintances. It is often after someone has received life-altering news. I pray for that healing; I pray for miraculous, complete, in-your-face, perfect healing. These prayers are usually focused on someone's physical healing, and that is the scale by which I have measured the success of my prayers. Did they live or did they die? It appears pretty straightforward. However, this doesn't leave any room to see growth on the journey. Someone who finds he or she is facing darkness may suddenly, miraculously, turn toward the light. They may experience profound spiritual healing, relationships restored, and forgiveness—offered or received—before they win or lose their fight. We need to notice these miracles, big and small, and rejoice in them along the way.

Perhaps this is the most important aspect of the healing that God is offering. As for myself, I have found there is a clarity that comes during tough times. Life, in its truest essence, emerges from the rubble as we cling to all that really matters: faith, family, fellowship, and the love that resides therein. Maybe an extended illness, while appearing horrible in every aspect to our human way of thinking, allows the opportunity for precious gifts to be received or given. I have seen what I know in my core to be miraculous physical healing without any evidence of spiritual awakening. And I have seen people become the most beautiful reflections of Christ—of His love, His grace—during a battle lost.

Personal Reflection

God is GOOD ~ ALL the time!

Holey Joy, Wholly Loved

Aaron took his last final exam today! Let me repeat: *Aaron took his last final exam today!* Almost everyone who knows Aaron knows that he has never been a big fan of anything scholastic. In fact, the last time I remember him enjoying school was in 4K, the second time through. He always did well, excelled in some classes and struggled through others, but he has never enjoyed the journey.

When he told me he had finished, there was the expected rush of emotion and jubilation that one would anticipate at the end of a hard-won battle. Yes! Fist pump! What I didn't see coming? The tears. Those caught me off guard—his tears, my tears, happy tears, wistful tears, missing you tears. It was like our joy had a hole right there in the center of it. A heart-shaped hole in our very present joy. Through that heart-shaped hole came a rush of love and memories and pride. Yes, we were able to feel wholly loved amid our holey joy. What a blessing!

Personal Reflection

God is GOOD ~ ALL the time!

Beautiful Tragedy

Last week I read this in my *One-Thousand Gifts Devotional* by Ann Voskamp:

> You may suffer loss but in Me is anything ever lost, really? Isn't everything that belongs to Christ also yours? Loved ones lost still belong to Him—then aren't they still yours? Aren't all provisions in Christ, also yours? If you haven't lost Christ, child, nothing is ever lost. Remember "through many tribulations we must enter the kingdom of God." (Acts 14:22)[24]

This idea has been floating around in my consciousness since I read it. I have reread it multiple times. The, "through many tribulations," part can be a bit off-putting, a little scary sounding. One thing that I have found during this journey, however, is that I have lost fear. I have encountered God in such a profound way during this time that I know with everything I am, no matter what tribulations I may encounter, He has got me. I have always said that faith and fear cannot coexist; I now believe that in my soul. I find this part of the reading to be so comforting: "If you haven't lost Christ, child, nothing is ever lost." Since John died, I have felt a spiritual connection to him that I cannot explain. It is breathtaking; it is a gift. And I am thankful for it. Living thankful, thanks filled, is something I was focusing on in my faith walk before losing John. I felt Christ's presence in very real and new ways.

I have found that having this mindset on my journey of grief has made every difference for me. I still search for beauty in the world. Today I stood silent in the woods. The shade and soft breeze offered a cool respite. The ground looked like it was covered in snow from the seeds of the cottonwoods overhead. The water lapped at the shore after turtles had plop, plop, plopped into the river. A startled owl swooped silently into the woods. I was in wonder. And I gave thanks. John was in the midst of that moment with me. "If you haven't lost Christ, child, nothing is ever lost."

Recently at our small-group retreat, one of my friends took my hand and looked into my eyes. She smiled, and with tears pooling, she said, "Whenever I see you, I still see him." Isn't that the beautiful tragedy of a love well lived and never lost?

Personal Reflection

God is GOOD ~ ALL the time!

Musings at 0330

God occasionally awakens me during the early morning hours, usually around 3:30. It is often under the guise of having to pee, at which point He says, "Now that I have your attention, I thought you might like to lift these people in prayer." Or, and this is my favorite, "Let's just ponder the ways of the universe for a while." This morning was a "pondering the universe," or more specifically, "pondering salvation" kind of chat. It started out simply by praying for a friend who recently lost his sister to cancer. When I spoke with him this week, I sensed he felt relief in that she was now in a much better place after having suffered for such a long time. There was a peace with her passing. But this made me think about those of us who have lost loved ones suddenly, in the blink of an eye. Peace and relief were not my first reactions. "You gotta be kidding me, God, really?" was more like it. Yet as I thought about it this morning, those who are taken quickly are perhaps doubly blessed. They go from joy to joy. No suffering, no aging, just a fast pass to paradise. That had never occurred to me before. What's hard is being left behind, trying to make sense of God's perfect timing, trying to find your way in a world that seems much darker.

In my GriefShare group we recently discussed heaven. The video we watched presented many perspectives about what heaven would be like. Ultimately, it is portrayed as being way better than here, indescribably so. We went on to discuss the stress one could have if their loved one wasn't a believer. I am not in this category as I am certain that if heaven is for real, then John Grant is there, probably running some part of it! I realize this certainty in John's salvation is a blessing that brings me abundant peace. However, what if I didn't have that confidence? I have always thought that only God knows the final utterances of one's heart.

That brought up the discussion in our group about deathbed conversions. Some people thought that it wasn't very fair. Live your life doing everything exactly like you want, then at the last second, proclaim your faith. They acted like it was somehow cheating. My thought is that it is actually very sad for that person to have never had the benefit of walking through life with Jesus. I think having to work out life in my Julie-sized mind would leave me feeling empty and so stressed. I am perfectly fine thinking that I am not ultimately responsible for pretty much anything of import, with faith in a plan that is so much bigger and more meaningful than mine. I really can't think of anything that I refrain from doing because I am a believer, but I can think of multiple things that I get out of journeying with Jesus. Peace and joy, grace and hope just to name a few. I require a lot of grace!

Then my mind went to the many conversations John and I had about faith, forgiveness, salvation, and even heaven. We both wondered about the salvation of nonbelievers who have never been introduced to Christ. Usually we think about someone in a jungle somewhere or in extreme isolation. If we think about it in the context of a developed country, we might think of someone raised in extreme poverty or neglect. But another thought occurred to me this morning. There are people all around us who perhaps have never truly been introduced to Christ. They may have heard His name, may have even gone to church, but sadly they never encountered Christ manifested in this world through us. They may have been exposed to the idols of money and power and status in their homes, but never to a servant's heart. So my prayer is that I might be used to show Christ to others, however He chooses I do that. If God wants me to go to the far reaches of the world, I am fine with that. But for now, maybe just trying to bring His light to my little corner of the world will suffice. I trust in His perfect plan for my life. Then when I read my morning devotion, it came together:

> You are the source of all life, and because of your light we
> see the light. (Psalm 36:9)

Personal Reflection

God is GOOD ~ ALL the time!

Precious Moments

Walking on the beach this morning, I had to fight the impulse to run up to the walking couples I encountered and tell them, "Stop! Take this in, all of it! The sun on your faces, the wind at your back, the smell of the sea, and your love walking with you." I wanted to remind them that these ordinary moments are precious, fleeting. These are the times that they may someday miss the most.

And then so many precious memories rushed through my heart, overflowing my eyes. It occurred to me that *this* moment is precious, fleeting, for me as well. Even though I am walking without my sweet man, I still have opportunities each day to be fully engaged in the present beauty of this life. As I gathered all of this into my heart, the waves deposited a sea-soaked feather at my feet. Feathers have come to me at amazing times and in all manner of ways. They are reminders from above. So I snatched up that tear-drenched feather and smiled and sang and even held out my arms to embrace the wind. Today is the perfect day to learn to fly.

> I have learned to be content in every situation. (Philippians 4:12)

Personal Reflection

God is GOOD ~ ALL the time!

The Gift of Being Present

On one of my hikes recently, I found myself smiling. Alone in the woods, walking, pondering, and grinning like a goofball, I thought, *I am happy. I am strong. I am joy-filled.* What a blessing that is! Yet there was something more: It was the realization that I was profoundly present in that very moment. I realized, maybe for the first time since John's death, that every thought, every step, every action, every breath is no longer filtered through the lens of grief. I am able to experience life with a purer clarity. From the discovery of deer tracks and blossoms on my path to spotting a leaf descending silently, twirling through the woods, from the barred owls calling to one another across the river to marveling at the color of the bluest sky, I am present! What a gift!

I don't think my joy in this moment in any way diminishes the height of the love that I shared with John, or the depth of the loss that has been endured. Rather, I think it is a great display of the love that our Father has for us in helping us to navigate the many valleys we must traverse in this life. If a gift has emerged from this valley, it is the realization that my world has become so much more closely intertwined with the spiritual realm, which is everywhere and within simultaneously. My faith has become a clearer lens through which to view life and loss. God has come so much nearer. In the words of Tozer, "We need never shout across the spaces to an absent God. He is nearer than our own soul, closer than our most secret thoughts." What a blessed assurance that is. This Friday will mark two years without John. As that day approaches, I am certain that the waves of grief will crash and probably crash hard. But I will be completely present then too, giving in to poignant surrender, certain that God will shelter me in this storm as well.

Whoever dwells in the shelter of the Most High will rest in the shadow of the Almighty. I will say of the Lord, "He is my refuge and my fortress, my God, in whom I trust." Surely, he will save you from the fowler's snare and from deadly pestilence. He will cover you with his feathers, and under his wings you will find refuge; (Psalm 91:1–4)

Personal Reflection

God is GOOD ~ ALL the time!

Paths of Love and Remembrance

I went on a bit of a pilgrimage while on my annual beach getaway this year. I had wanted to scatter some of John's ashes at the end of the long jetty at one of our favorite beaches. As soon as I started across the causeway, the memories and tears flooded in. So many sweet memories. Our last visit was about three months before John died. We had stopped with his mom on the way home from Myrtle Beach. I ventured out onto the trail that leads to an observation point, camera in hand. On the way back I had stopped, taking in the scent of jasmine and blossoms scattered all over the trail. I was just quietly breathing it all in when I looked up and saw John standing on the trail about fifteen feet away, just watching me and smiling. That smile revealed his dimples and crept to his eyes. I called him a sexy voyeur, and we laughed and enjoyed a long hug in the shelter of the pines, wrapped in wafting jasmine.

This was the first beach John took me to when we moved to South Carolina. It was one of his favorite places from his trips to the area as a college student. I was pregnant with Daniel, and John insisted on me waddling the entire mile to the jetty. It was worth it. The sea was a beautiful blue-green color, and the waves were crashing on both sides, spraying us with a cool mist. We often stopped there with the kids as they grew, looking for alligators, running along the boardwalks, and always making our way to the jetty. I knew I needed to leave a part of him there.

I listened to music and prayed that God would reveal the perfect place. I kept my eyes alert for feathers, always a sign of God being near me. Out on the jetty, shafts of light were pouring from the clouds, and I turned in time to see three little birds just pop out of nowhere and appear on a rock. Three little birds—this must be the place. As I quietly sat there, I noticed the tiniest feather, about the size of my pinky fingernail, stuck on the rock. I reached to free it from the rock, and the wind immediately pulled it from my hand and lifted it skyward. I sighed.

As I stepped from the jetty and back onto the beach, I noticed a very bedraggled, water-soaked feather. Smiling, I picked it up for my collection of important feathers. For about a half a mile, I don't think I went more than five or ten steps without seeing another feather right at the water's edge. Truly gifts from the sea. "Show off," I said aloud to God, grinning big.

It has been over two years since John died. I have mostly good days. There are still days that sting and times I lean into my grief and loss. I think when you are traveling on a grief-shadowed journey, you occasionally need to walk those paths of love and remembrance with the fresh legs of hope in order to truly grasp just how far the Lord has carried you. I don't know what the future holds, but I do know who holds my future, and I know with everything I am that He is good.

> But I'm in the very presence of God—oh, how refreshing it is! I've made Lord God my home. God, I'm telling the world what you do! (Psalm 73:28 The Message)

Personal Reflection

God is GOOD ~ ALL the time!

Notes

1   Tenth Avenue North, "By Your Side." https://genius.com/Tenth-Avenue-North-By-Your-Side-lyrics, accessed April 14, 2019.

2   Matthew West, "Broken Things." https://genius.com/Matthew-West-Broken-Things-lyrics, accessed July 17, 2018.

3   Hillary Scott, "Thy Will." https://genius.com/Hillary-Scott-Thy Will-lyrics, accessed August 11, 2018.

4   Third Day, "Cry Out to Jesus." https://genius.com/Third-Day-Cry-Out-To-Jesus-lyrics, accessed August 23, 2018.

5   Casting Crowns, "Somewhere in the Middle." https://genius.com/Casting-Crowns-Somewhere-In-The-Middle-lyrics, accessed September 30, 2018.

6   Henri J. M. Nouwen, *The Inner Voice of Love* (New York: Image Books Doubleday, 1998), 63–64.

7   Sarah Young, *Jesus Calling* (Nashville: Thomas Nelson, 2013), 88.

8   Hillsong United, "Oceans." https://genius.com/Hillsong-United-Oceans-lyrics, accessed July 30, 2018.

9   Young, *Jesus Calling*, 100.

10 Sidewalk Prophets, "Keep Making Me." https://genius.com/Sidewalk-Prophets-Keep-Making-Me-lyrics, accessed November 27, 2018.

11 Young, *Jesus Calling*, 324.

12 Lauren Daigle, "Trust in You." https://genius.com/Lauren-Daigle-Trust-In-You-lyrics, accessed September 22, 2018.

13 Ann Voskamp, *The Way of Abundance* (Grand Rapids: Zondervan, 2012), 141.

14 Danny Gokey, "Tell Your Heart to Beat Again." https://genius.com/Danny-Gokey-Tell-Your-Heart-To-Beat-Again-lyrics, accessed July 22, 2018.

15 "Faith," *Merriam-Webster*, accessed March 20, 2019, https://www.merriam-webster.com/dictionary/faith.

16 Martha Whitmore Hickman, *Healing After Loss* (New York: Harper Collings, 1994), January 3.

17 Ann Voskamp, *One Thousand Gifts Devotional* (Grand Rapids: Zondervan, 2012), 172.

18 Casting Crowns, "Just Be Held." https://genius.com/Casting-Crowns-Just-Be-Held-lyrics, accessed March 1, 2020.

19 Casting Crowns, "The Well." https://genius.com/Casting-Crowns-The-Well-lyrics, accessed January 23, 2019

20 John Eldredge, *Restoration Year* (Nashville: Thomas Nelson, 2018), 26.

21 Young, *Jesus Calling*, 321.

22 Jason Gray, "With Every Act of Love." https://genius.com/Jason-Gray-With-Ever y-Act-Of-Love-lyrics, accessed August 28, 2018.

23 Mikeschair, "Someone Worth Dying For." https://genius.com/Mikeschai r-Someone-Worth-Dying-For-lyrics, accessed November 16, 2018.

24 Voskamp, *One Thousand Gifts Devotional*, 91.

GriefShare is a network of 15,000+ churches worldwide equipped to offer grief support groups. The program is nondenominational and features biblical concepts for healing from your grief. Learn more about GriefShare at www.GriefShare.org.